Understanding Jesus Today

THE WORLD OF JESUS

Understanding Jesus Today

Edited by Howard Clark Kee

Growing interest in the historical Jesus can be frustrated by diverse and conflicting claims about what he said and did. This series brings together in accessible form the conclusions of an international team of distinguished scholars regarding various important aspects of Jesus' teaching. All of the authors have extensively analyzed the Biblical and contextual evidence about who Jesus was and what he taught, and they summarize their findings here in easily readable and stimulating discussions. Each book includes an appendix of questions for further thought and recommendations for further reading on the topic covered.

Other Books in the Series

Howard Clark Kee, *What Can We Know About Jesus?*
Pheme Perkins, *Jesus as Teacher*
David Tiede, *Jesus and the Future*

The World of Jesus

First-Century Judaism in Crisis

JOHN RICHES

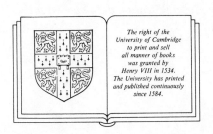

The right of the
University of Cambridge
to print and sell
all manner of books
was granted by
Henry VIII in 1534.
The University has printed
and published continuously
since 1584.

CAMBRIDGE UNIVERSITY PRESS
Cambridge
New York Port Chester Melbourne Sydney

Published by the Press Syndicate of the University of Cambridge
The Pitt Building, Trumpington Street, Cambridge CB2 1RP
40 West 20th Street, New York, NY 10011, USA
10 Stamford Road, Oakleigh, Melbourne 3166, Australia

First published 1990
Reprinted 1991

Printed in the United States of America

Library of Congress Cataloging-in-Publication Data
Riches, John Kenneth.
The world of Jesus.
(Understanding Jesus today)
Includes bibliographical references (p.   ) and index.
1. Judaism – History – Post-exilic period, 586 B.C.–
210 A.D. 2. Bible. N.T. Gospels – History of contem-
porary events. I. Title. II. Series.
BM176.R53 1990   290′.09′015   90–2410

ISBN 0–521–38505–9 hardback
ISBN 0–521–38676–4 paperback

British Library cataloguing in publication data applied for

Contents

86859

Introduction

Great religious prophets and innovators transcend their time. They reach out beyond it, perceiving new worlds and new times beyond the imaginings of their contemporaries. They evoke in some of their contemporaries a response that sets them on the difficult and problematic task of transposing such dreams into reality. The Protestant Reformation gives birth to modern Europe; early Christianity dons the imperial robe.

Such religious figures, however, remain in one sense on their own. Standing at the margins of their society, isolated from the rest of their contemporaries, they dream dreams that bring down the wrath of the powers that be and cause their friends to wonder if they have taken leave of their senses. Luther stands alone at Worms to face the might of the Holy Roman Empire of the German Nation. Jesus dies on the cross abandoned by even his closest followers.

And so it is tempting for the prophets' later followers to wrest them out of their time altogether, to see them and their words as belonging no longer to their original setting but as eternally destined for all peoples and societies. We study the texts that report their words and deeds as if they spoke equally clearly to all people at all times. The text becomes the thing. But in setting the text free from its time, the prophets' followers run the risk of divorcing the texts, not only from their contemporary setting but from the prophets themselves.

And this will not do. However much some prophetic figures transcend their time, they do so precisely as men and women of their time. Standing at the doorway into a new world, they

1

nonetheless share their contemporaries' hopes and fears and seek to lead their people out into what is to come. Their words speak to their contemporaries' condition: They may meet with opposition and incomprehension, but they also address their people's deepest hopes and desires. In their preaching and their deeds they seek to transform people's understanding of themselves and their world and prepare them to embrace the world to come. It is in this interaction with traditional, inherited beliefs and practices that they are able to exercise their extraordinary power over their contemporaries. And it is in this that their power to create new worlds resides.

For this reason study of the biblical texts about Jesus needs to set them back into their contemporary context. If we want to understand how these texts may serve to transform our own situation, then it may be of help to see how Jesus' words and deeds were able to transform his own world and indeed to produce the texts the church was subsequently to canonize.

But what kind of context do we need to explore? Often in this kind of quest the context has been conceived of fairly narrowly as a literary one: We need to know as much as we can about other contemporary Jewish texts in order to understand what Jesus was saying. There is nothing wrong about that in itself; there is danger only if we divorce those writings from their context in the life and history of the Jewish people, just as we have tended to divorce the biblical texts from their own particular historical context. Then we shall treat these ancient texts merely as sources for other religious doctrines of that time, with which to compare and contrast Jesus' teaching. And we shall fail to ask how those doctrines related to the actual lives, hopes, and fears of the Jewish people.

To give an example, a great deal of attention has been given to Jewish apocalyptic literature at the turn of the era. This literature, starting with Daniel in the second century B.C. and including great collections like 1 Enoch, contains visions of a catastrophe that will bring in the final age. It is full of doctrines about how this future world will come, some of which bear striking resemblance to ideas found in the New Testament. One way of relating Jesus' teaching to this kind of text is simply to compare and contrast: Jesus speaks about the coming of the kingdom "with power" but does not engage in speculation about when this will be, rejecting calls for signs of its coming. Apocalyptic literature gives much richer portrayals of the end and also speculates vigorously about the "times," how much longer there is before the end arrives, and how God's people will be able to recognize the crucial moments. Similarly we may choose to contrast different views about the nature of the Messiah, or similar savior figures referred to in these texts.

That is all very well so far as it goes. Indeed, it is most important work. But we shall not come to understand very much about why there are these similarities and differences between Jesus and contemporary seers, unless we understand more about how this body of literature relates to the situation of the Jews at the time. Under what conditions did people begin to dream such strange dreams of future torment and rescue? How did such hopes – and fears – relate to the political and social aspirations of an occupied people? How did they relate to more traditional Jewish beliefs? Why did Jews find it necessary to modify or recast their traditional beliefs at all?

The answer to these questions, I want to suggest, can only be found if we first take a much closer look at the economic, social, and political setting of such texts. We need to see texts like the apocalyptic texts as responses to an ongoing history of national struggle for independence and for the preservation of traditional Jewish religious practices and beliefs. And the same goes for other contemporary texts and doctrines.

The emergence of great religious figures can hardly ever be purely accidental, independent, that is, of the historical constellation under which they are born. They are figures who mark the great cultural shifts in the history of the human race. But they are not simply products of such shifts: Their greatness lies in the way in which they set their own stamp on them, laying the foundations for a host of cultural constructions in following generations.

Certainly it is true that Jesus emerges at a critical turning point in the history of the Jewish people, as indeed of the whole Mediterranean world. Within forty years of his death the heart of contemporary Judaism, the Temple, was destroyed. Out of that disaster arose, on the one hand, rabbinic Judaism and, on the other, Christianity. But at the same time that disaster in Jerusalem was itself part of a wider phenomenon Jews could ignore only at their peril, namely, the creation of the Roman principate. The resolution of the civil war between Anthony and Octavian in 30 B.C. meant that Palestine became, willy-nilly, part of a larger and largely cohesive political unit. As a religious group Jews had effectively three choices: They could seek to break the grip of Roman power; they could choose to retreat into a form of communal piety, accommodating where necessary to the political realities of Roman rule; or they could attempt to convert Rome.

It is interesting to reflect that, out of the many religious groups and movements that flourished in the Mediterranean in the first century, only two would survive in any substantial institutionalized form, and both had their roots in the crisis in first-century Palestine.

But how far can Jesus be held responsible for what came after him? Even if we succeed in showing him as the kind of prophetic figure who points his people to a coming new age, what is it to say that he set his stamp on it? How far can he be held responsible for the great diversity of forms that Christianity, through the ages, has taken?

Of course this is a massive question that we cannot hope to answer adequately. For the purposes of this book what I want to say is this: All cultures are sustained by certain basic beliefs that may, however, be articulated and expressed in a variety of ways. This, as we shall see, was certainly true of Judaism. Belief in the Covenant between God and Israel and in the Law as the expression of God's will was basic to most Jews most of the time. Yet when pressed, those who held such beliefs could articulate them in many different ways, and this gave rise to fierce debate and antagonism. In the same way the many different cultural manifestations of Christianity are all predicated on certain basic beliefs about God's act of salvation in Christ, and yet Christian history too is proof of the way in which different understandings of these basic beliefs have given rise to very different forms of social and cultural life.

What is Jesus' place in all this? It can hardly be said that he himself laid down the basic beliefs that would sustain Christianity through the ages. Insofar as they concern his death and resurrection it must be clear that such a framework of belief was the work of his followers, the Evangelists and Paul, more than of Jesus. And yet that is not all there is to be said. As we shall see, there is an important sense in which Jesus is already beginning to suggest significant modifications in Jewish beliefs. In one sense this may not go as far as challenging basic beliefs in the Law and the Covenant: Such matters were still being vigorously debated in the church at the time of Paul and Matthew, some twenty to fifty years after Jesus' death. What he does, I shall suggest, is to challenge certain modes of articulating belief in God's governance of the world, certain understandings of justice and goodness, which, once pressed, will have far-reaching consequences. It is the radical nature of Jesus' understanding of God's Rule that will cause Paul to start talking about an old and a new Covenant, or to begin to work out some view of the Law that can see it both as superseded and yet as having played a part in God's purposes for his world.

One of the fascinating things about the Christian tradition is the way that it has always retained this uneasy relationship with the "Old" Covenant. Rather than having received an unequivocal set of basic beliefs from a "founder," Christianity received as its heritage a series of stories and sayings that place it in a seemingly unending dialogue with the rich and complex traditions of Israel.

Attempts to resolve this dialogue by breaking it off have been resisted. When the second-century Christian scholar Marcion rejected the ancient Jewish writings and indeed part of the Christian Scriptures as well, the church rejected him. But the church has also resisted efforts to absorb Jesus and his teaching within the Old Covenant, as was attempted by certain forms of Jewish Christianity. Rather, by canonizing the "Old" Testament along with the New, the church has given it a normative position within the community and has ensured the continuity of that dialogue. Thus Jesus remains as it were one voice in the Christian church's continuing dialogue. It is an ongoing dialogue and its products in the various forms of church and social life remain always provisional, always subject to revision and modification.

What I want to suggest through this study of Jesus in his contemporary context is that this unending dialogue cannot be seen simply as an intellectual, theological dialogue without relevance to its contemporary social, economic, and political context. Christian theology cannot for long abstract from the practical questions of its implications for social and political life. The context of Jesus' preaching and teaching in the continuing struggle and search of the Jewish people for self-determination should make that clear. In this sense true Christian theology must always be contextual.

In this volume of the series my task is specifically to examine the ways in which Jewish figures and groups of the first century, Jesus included, reacted to the basic social, economic and political realities of the time. Accordingly I shall attempt to show how Jesus' prophetic activity represents one among a number of first-century Jewish responses to the prolonged political and cultural pressures to which they had been subjected. And it will be an important part of this task to show how all these responses spring from the same stock of Jewish belief in God's covenantal rule.

We shall begin then in Chapter 1 by attempting to give an account of the social, economic, political, and cultural context within which Jesus and other Jewish leaders operated. And we shall look briefly too at the wider Hellenistic culture that permeated the whole of the Mediterranean world, as it had done with varying degrees of acceptance and rejection since Alexander's campaigns in the fourth century B.C.

Before turning to a specific investigation of first-century Jewish groups, however, we need to look in Chapter 2 at the common stock of beliefs on which such groups drew, in virtue of which they could all be said to be Jewish – and at the already quite different forms that those beliefs had been given in the last two centuries B.C. That diversity is itself the expression of different responses to Israel's changing situation and therefore constitutes part of the cultural resources on which Jews of the first century could draw as they grappled with their own particular problems.

Chapters 3–5 then examine the main Jewish movements and groups in the early part of the first century A.D., including Jesus himself. Rather than discuss each group on its own, I have chosen a fairly simple set of questions to put one by one to the various groups, which then makes it possible to compare the respective answers at each stage.

I start, in Chapter 3, by asking how a group defines its membership. Rules and marks of membership, whether or not formalized, may be interestingly informative of a group's central concerns and values. To ask how a group defines membership is, it should be noticed, not quite the same as asking how a member gets in. That suggests too easily an element of choice and deliberate initiation, which although it may have been important for some Jews was not so for those who stressed membership through birth and infant circumcision. The question, that is, of how far some deliberate, voluntary act of subscribing to the group was necessary before one could consider oneself a member of God's people was itself contentious.

In Chapter 4 I shall inquire into the various strategies Jewish groups of the time devised to help their members uphold group norms and values. For some this involved a redefinition, in part at least, of traditional Jewish norms, or the emphasizing of parts of the tradition at the cost of others. For some it involved devising patterns of group activity that reinforced members' determination to uphold the traditional norms in their entirety. These are not, of course, mutually exclusive ways: The redefinition of norms and the development of disciplinary strategies may go hand in hand.

And then, in Chapter 5, I shall ask what vision of and hopes for the future were shared by each of the groups. The question is particularly relevant in a situation where the existing state of affairs is regarded as in some sense abnormal – contrary, that is, to God's will. What is interesting to note here is that the views held by any one group may differ considerably. It seems indeed likely that views of the future were the product of individual seers, which were then subsequently espoused with varying degrees of tenacity by particular groups at different times. This is certainly true of the early Christian community.

In all this we shall of course be concerned not simply to give a mere listing of the different ways in which various groups dealt with such questions. Rather in comparing and contrasting the different answers we shall be considering them as more or less intelligible responses to the complex historical situation in which such groups found themselves and which we will have attempted to describe in Chapters 1 and 2. Thus in an age

in which some Jews by birth saw it as politic to make some
accommodation with their received norms and standards in
order to coexist and cooperate with an alien occupying power,
others may have found it necessary to define membership of
the group no longer principally in terms of birth and circumcision but of active and conscious espousal of Jewish norms.
Again groups that link their identity strongly with the holding
of certain sharply defined beliefs, their preservation, cultivation, and implementation, may need to devise defensive strategies to protect themselves from the infiltration of heterodox
beliefs into the community. And I suspect that the fluctuation
in beliefs about the future even within individual groups will
have related partly to the extent to which they believed the
alien forces in society were firmly entrenched and partly to the
amount of power they themselves could command. If nothing
short of a major upheaval could remove the foreign power then
groups with little or no power would be likely to look for some
divine act of intervention, while those more powerful would
harbor visions of a successful holy war, though even here they
might hope for some final divine act of intervention.

Once we have offered such a comparative account of the
various Jewish responses to the crisis of first-century Palestine
we should be better able to grasp the nature of Jesus' own
vision and message, to which we shall devote Chapter 6. Our
previous discussion should enable us the better to see it as a
distinctive yet analogous response to the perplexing realities
that troubled others of his contemporaries. This in turn may
enable us to discern something of its remarkable power to
transform his followers' understanding of themselves and their
world.

The Political, Economic, Social, and Cultural Context of First-Century Palestinian Judaism

What were the political, economic, social, and cultural forces that affected everyday life in Roman Palestine in the first century? What was their history and how in practice were such forces experienced by ordinary Jews? Were they experienced as bearable, desirable, offering opportunities for fulfillment; or as oppressive, posing severe obstacles to the development of a truly Jewish way of life? These questions are complex, and the answers given here are necessarily abbreviated.

The Political Situation

Developments up to the Beginning of the First Century and the Pax Augusta

Palestine at the turn of the era was under Roman control. It was not, however, all controlled in the same manner. Herod the Great, a loyal and politically crafty client king, had just died (4 B.C.). His kingdom, after much deliberation by Augustus at Rome, had been divided between his three sons, Archelaus, Philip, and Herod Antipas. Archelaus was appointed ethnarch over Judea, Samaria, and Idumaea; Herod Antipas tetrarch over Galilee and Peraea; Herod Philip tetrarch over Batanaea, Trachonitis, and Auranitis (*Ant.* xvii.317–20). None received the title "king," which they wanted, though the title "ethnarch" had more dignity than that of tetrarch. Within a few years Archelaus' disastrous rule would end in the imposition of direct Roman rule over Judea (A.D. 6). Herod Antipas' rule in

Galilee would last until he incurred the emperor Caligula's (A.D. 37–41) displeasure in A.D. 39 by asking to be made king (*Ant.* xviii.240–55). By A.D. 44 all Palestine was directly administered by a Roman procurator.

Looked at from the vantage of Rome these events were no more than minor administrative adjustments in the long process of forging a united Mediterranean world. In the last decades of the fourth century B.C., Alexander the Great had dominated the East from Macedonia to India. Rome had come to power slowly. First it established control over the western Mediterranean, wresting power from Carthage in a series of wars (264–41; 218–201; 149–46 B.C.) that culminated in the establishment of the Roman province of Africa. From this position Rome could turn its attention eastward. In the first century B.C., Pompey, in a series of spectacular campaigns, won victories in Africa (81), Spain (72), cleared the Mediterranean of pirates (67), and finally imposed Roman rule in Asia (long troubled by wars with Mithradites, d. 63), Syria, and Judea (66–63). The final prize was secured when after the civil war between Mark Anthony and Octavian (Mark Anthony was defeated at the Battle of Actium, 31 B.C.), Cleopatra's Egypt, with its vitally important supplies of grain, became a Roman province (30 B.C.).

The old republican form of government was discarded. Octavian, now to be known as Augustus, emerged as the emperor of the Mediterranean world and inaugurated the *pax augusta*. Trade routes were secured. A system of roads, post, and communications covered the area. An effective and largely equitable system of provincial administration was instituted. Conditions of travel improved. In a very real sense Augustus brought peace and prosperity to the Mediterranean, at least for those who were able and willing to take the opportunities he offered.

How far Jews were able to share this view of things no doubt varied considerably. Jews in the Hellenistic cities of North Af-

rica, Syria, and Asia Minor may well have welcomed the greater political stability and improved opportunities for trade and
the development of their own communities. Perhaps there
were Jews in Palestine who saw things this way too. Yet for
those Jews in Palestine who stood to gain little but further
changes in the pattern of foreign domination and taxation it
will have looked very different. For them the coming of the
Romans was but one further episode in the continuing history
of the invasion and colonization of their country.

That history was as old as their own occupation of the land
itself. It had had its low points: the Exile, the imposition of
direct foreign rule after Alexander's campaigns in the fourth
century, the desecration of the Temple by Antiochus Epiphanes, the Syrian king (in 169 B.C.), and again in 63 B.C., the
conferring of Roman provincial status on the country after
Pompey's desecration of the Temple. It had also had its moments of triumph, most notably with the successful uprising
against Antiochus under the Maccabees (166–159 B.C.). This
led ultimately to the establishment of a Jewish dynasty, the
Hasmoneans (140–37 B.C.), and inaugurated a period of expansion. It was at this time toward the end of John Hyrcanus' reign
(134–104 B.C.) that Galilee again came under Jewish rule. But
however much independence Jews gained, in the end Jewish
rulers had to take into account the realities of power in the
Mediterranean world. And this meant foreign diplomacy and
adopting foreign ways, molding one's attitudes and institutions
to the ways of the surrounding world.

It is of course hard to know how far Jews in rural Galilee, say,
were aware of the details of this history. Stories of heroic resistance to foreign invaders were known and celebrated: David
and Goliath were presumably at least as popular then as now.
More recent heroes like Judas Maccabeus (killed in battle in
160 B.C.; see 1 Mc 9) and his family were also remembered, not
least in the festival of Hannukah, which celebrated Judas' re-

possession of the Temple (164 B.C.; 1 Mc 4:36–51). At the same time there were darker images of exile and destruction that were also remembered in readings and in psalms (Ps 137). Along with these images and stories from the past went more recent memories. From Nazareth Jesus could see the city of Sepphoris, which had been burned and captured by Roman forces during the revolt after the death of Herod (4 B.C.). Its inhabitants were sold into slavery, while in the aftermath of the troubles, Varus, the Roman governor of Syria, sought out the instigators and crucified two thousand. Sepphoris was being rebuilt at the time of Jesus and had become a key city in the region, "the ornament of all Galilee" (*Ant.* xviii.27; see also xvii.271–2, 289, 295).

Firm evidence for popular attitudes to this history is naturally hard to come by. What we do know is that the period from the time of Pompey to the First Jewish War (63 B.C.–A.D. 70) was marked by a steady series of uprisings. Only in the period from A.D. 6 to 40 was there relative quiet. The exception to this were the disturbances in A.D. 6 occasioned by Quirinius' census in Judea. Initial protests in Jerusalem were quietened by the intervention of the high priest. But Judas the Galilean, together with a Pharisee, Saddok, stirred up trouble in the north, which Josephus sees as the start of the troubles that ultimately led to the Jewish War (*Ant.* xvii.271–7). Serious trouble was again threatened in A.D. 39–41 by Caligula's attempts to set up his statue in the Temple. This was averted, however, by careful stalling tactics on the part of the Roman governor (*Ant.* xviii.261–304).

Nevertheless such disturbances were rare in the first four decades of the century. Whether this was due to the harshness with which the risings after Herod's death were put down or to the relative firmness and mildness of Antipas' rule in Galilee (4 B.C.–A.D. 39) is more difficult to say. However that may be, this period of quiet was not without its undercurrents. It was after all the time of John the Baptist and of Jesus, both of whom aroused widespread hopes of an imminent end to the world. That suggests that popular feeling was easily stirred by hopes of a release from prevailing conditions.

Roman Provincial Administration and Client Kingdoms

Like many colonial powers, Rome did not adopt a uniform pattern of administration of the territories it controlled. It found the arrangement that worked best and, if it caused problems, changed it. If a local ruler could be found who was competent and would be loyal to Rome, then he would be used. Herod the Great, though a powerful king in the eyes of the Jews, owed his position entirely to Roman support. He was first declared king of Judaea in Rome at a formal meeting of the senate in 40 B.C. He owed this to Mark Anthony, who saw him as a useful ally in his struggle against the Parthians who were in turn supported by the then Hasmonean king, Antigonus (*Ant.* xiv.381–93). Herod had to wait three years before he was able to take possession of his kingdom. Then, with the help of the Roman army under Sossius, he stormed Jerusalem, slaughtering many of his subjects in the process. And it was only by offering gifts that he was able to call off the Roman soldiers from ransacking and desecrating the Temple (*Ant.* xiv.468–91). He nearly lost his kingdom again when he found himself on the losing side in the war between Octavian (Augustus) and Mark Anthony. However, his speed in traveling to Octavian to assure him of similar loyalty to that which he had shown to Anthony saved him (*Ant.* xv.187–201), and he remained in power to his death in 4 B.C. Any suggestion that a client ruler's loyalty might be less than absolute could lead to his deposition. When in A.D. 39 the tetrarch Herod Antipas asked the emperor Caligula to make him king, he was swiftly deposed despite his excellent record as a strong and effective ruler (*Ant.* xviii.240–55).

Part of the price for a client ruler's remaining in power was military cooperation with Rome. When Herod Antipas ruled in Galilee, Judea, to the south, was administered by a prefect ultimately responsible to the Roman governor in Syria, to the north. That is to say, the lines of communication ran straight through Antipas' territory. Roman troops marching from Damascus to Jerusalem would have passed along the military road not far from Nazareth. There was no question of respecting Galilee's sovereignty!

At the same time, the client ruler was in many cases expected to collect taxes for the Romans. This he would have done by whatever system suited him, most often some form of tax farming, rather than the direct levy of a poll tax. Sometimes this obligation could be relaxed, as it probably was in the latter part of Herod the Great's reign (as is suggested by Herod's ability to remit taxes to his own subjects, *Ant.* xv.365). It is likely, however, that it was reimposed after his death, though with the concession that his successors could draw an income for themselves, on which Augustus imposed strict limits (*Ant.* xvii.318ff.). This would most likely then have involved a measure of imperial supervision. The important point was that the emperor was heavily dependent on the taxes he received from the provinces for maintaining his own position.

But above all it was important that any client king should be able to maintain order. Archelaus, Herod the Great's son who ruled over Judea after Herod's death, was a disaster and was removed in A.D. 6 after a series of uprisings (*Ant.* xvii.342–4). This meant of course that Rome had to station more troops in Judea, and this was both expensive and politically dangerous. There were too many examples in Roman history of generals from the provinces wielding inordinate power and influence. Nevertheless by A.D. 44 all Palestine was administered directly as part of the Roman province of Syria. Doubtless in many ways this made good administrative sense.

But while it may have made better administrative sense, di-

rect Roman rule was not without its pitfalls. Judea after Archelaus' death was placed under a Roman governor whose main
headquarters were at Caesarea on the coast. The Roman garrison was based there, with forces also stationed in Jerusalem,
which would be reinforced at major festivals. The governors
were charged with collecting tribute as well as with admin-
istering law and order. Initially they were referred to as pre-
fects, stressing their military role; later they were called
procurators, which strictly refers to their financial responsibil-
ities. They were ultimately subject to the legate in Syria, but
this appears only to have taken force in times of crisis. Their
power and jurisdiction over all areas of life are well illustrated
by the fact that they could and did appoint and dismiss the high
priest at will.

They did not, however, always understand the particular sen-
sibilities of the Jews. Pontius Pilate (A.D. 26–36) offended on a
number of occasions, first by introducing standards into Jerusalem bearing embossed images of the emperor (which of course
violated the prohibition against graven images; *Ant.* xviii.55–
9). Further offense was given by his use of Temple funds to
construct an aqueduct in Jerusalem (*Ant.* xviii.60–2). Even
after this he attempted to introduce shields bearing the emperor's name into Jerusalem (Philo, *Embassy* 38.299–306). In
his handling of popular disturbances he was brutal, and eventually his harsh treatment of a Samaritan prophet and his followers led to his deposition (*Ant.* xviii.85–9).

Economic and Social Life in First-Century Palestine

Social Divisions in Ancient Society

Social divisions were differently marked in ancient society
than in modern industrial ones. Contemporary Western society
is divided into classes that are largely though not entirely de-

fined by reference to their position within an industrial economy: workers/management; shareholders/wage earners; employed/self-employed/unemployed. Although some of these distinctions would have applied in first-century societies, other distinctions were more important.

There was a crucial distinction between slave and free. Jews, because of their own history of liberation "from the house of slaves," disliked keeping slaves, particularly Jewish slaves, but some still kept them. The Romans needed huge numbers of slaves to support their economy. It is estimated that in Italy at the end of the republic there were some two million slaves. This represents about 35 percent of the population, which is a figure very similar to that obtaining in the southern United States before abolition. Thus slaves would have been a feature of life in Palestine, though perhaps something that most Jews viewed somewhat from a distance. Nevertheless the threat of being sold into slavery to redeem one's debts must have been a real one for many Jews (cf. Mt 18:25). Equally those who engaged in active revolt knew that slavery was one possible outcome. It was the fate of the survivors of the revolt in Sepphoris after Herod's death (*Ant.* xvii.289).

Second, there would be differences of birth. Clearly for Jews, being born and circumcised a Jew was of crucial significance. It was this that made one a member of the Covenant and defined one's whole existence by contrast, more or less sharp, with the Gentiles (Gn 17:9–14).

There were also distinctions the Jews made among themselves, not least between those who worshiped at Jerusalem and the Samaritans, who maintained that the true site of the Temple was on Mount Gerizim. The history of the rift dates back to struggles in the Persian period for control of Judah that resulted in the building of an alternative temple on Mount Gerizim toward the end of the fourth century B.C. The final breach came with its destruction by John Hyrcanus (134–104

B.C.). Samaritans harassed pilgrims going from the north to Jerusalem. They did not fight in the Jewish War, though they opposed the Romans on other occasions and suffered both under Pilate, as we have seen, and under Vespasian during the Jewish War (A.D. 66–70).

And, just as Jews distinguished themselves from Gentiles, so too inside and outside Palestine, in the Greek cities where there were substantial communities of Jews, they were distinguished from their fellow citizens. Sometimes this was accompanied by aggression and personal attack, as in A.D. 38 in Alexandria, where there were said to live a million Jews. This was occasioned by the Jews' wish to be granted full citizenship. The matter was eventually resolved by the subsequent emperor Claudius, who forbade Jews to participate in athletic contexts and told them to enjoy prosperity in a "city not their own." Those Jews, however, who had already achieved full citizenship (presumably only a minority) should remain as such. The implication is that the others were to be regarded as resident aliens, enjoying certain privileges but not to be admitted to the gymnasium (cf. *Ant.* xix.278–85).

Birth also determined one's rank in the family. In the first place, of course, gender determined roles and functions within the family and in society at large. First-century Palestine, like other surrounding societies, was thoroughly patriarchal. Birth also determined one's position in the hierarchy of the family, the firstborn male ranking above subsequent male offspring. And birth into particular families also determined membership of the priesthood. Only they could offer sacrifices at Jerusalem and thus they enjoyed a privileged if not necessarily wealthy position. The priests were divided into various groupings, and it is likely that the high priests were drawn only from certain of these groupings. Thus within the hierarchy there were important distinctions of status. In this respect Palestine was a hierarchical society.

There were other ways, however, of classifying people that depended not on birth but on language. Ever since the military campaigns of Alexander had brought Hellenistic culture to the East, the ability to speak Greek had been a passport to social status and power. One needed to speak Greek in order to enter the administrative ranks, to trade, to travel, to engage in diplomacy. Under the Romans Greek became a means of cementing together a large empire composed of many different and traditionally antagonistic peoples. We shall discuss this further later in the chapter.

Town and Country in Jewish Society

Perhaps the most important distinction in Jewish society was based on where one lived. A great gulf divided town and country. In many ways it must have been like the division between town and country in many parts of Africa today. The city population in Africa has different styles of life, different economic standards, is more international and Westernized than the rural population, which feels deeply estranged from what is effectively an alien and very powerful culture in its midst. So too in first-century Palestine the rural population must have felt itself to be largely cut off from the urban life of the country with its strong links to the Hellenistic world of the Mediterranean.

This distinction would have been marked out culturally, politically, legally, and economically. Many of the cities in Palestine bore names whose roots were Greek or Latin: Sebaste, Apollonia, Caesarea Panias, Tiberias, Caesarea Philippi, Julias. They were controlled by Greek-speaking merchants, officials, and landowners. Most people who lived in a city in Palestine would have been able to get by in Greek. Moreover in many cities the population would have been predominantly gentile, sometimes living in considerable tension with the Jewish community. Cities where the Jewish population was numerically strong might have to be garrisoned in times of political tension. Jamnia where, after the fall of Jerusalem, the Jewish Academy was established, had to be garrisoned twice by Vespasian (*War* iv.130, 444). Where Jews were in a minority they were, by contrast, extremely vulnerable at such times. At Caesarea, the seat of the Roman governor, the Jewish inhabitants were attacked by "the people of Caesarea," who slaughtered more than twenty thousand in an hour, which in turn provoked savage reprisals on other cities by Jewish raiding parties (*War* ii.457).

Politically the cities enjoyed a considerable measure of independence. They were ruled by councils entitled to make their own laws. Moreover their authority did not stop at the city boundaries but extended over the surrounding areas. Nevertheless their freedom had its limits. In general, cities paid taxes and supplied military forces to whatever major power controlled their area. The Jewish Hasmonean rulers gained control of many of the cities during their period of rule (140–37 B.C.). Pompey "liberated" these cities, which then, with exceptions, became loyal to Rome. The measure of freedom enjoyed by cities varied considerably. Some cities were granted autonomy and immunity from taxes. In practice there would always have been a certain tension between the cities' desire for independence and the overlords' wish to exercise control over their territories through the cities.

Economically, cities were centers of wealth, trade, and industry and the seat of many of the major landowners. In Palestine, Jerusalem, with its numerous pilgrims and visitors to the Temple, was the major center of wealth. It also boasted fine craftworkers in glassware, stone carving, and pottery and offered less sophisticated goods for the many thousands employed on public building works (*Ant.* xx.219). The coastal cities too were important centers of trade and commerce. Above all their wealth would have stood out in sharp contrast to the relative poverty of the surrounding rural areas. One important expression of this would have been in the architecture of the buildings. This architectural magnificence was to be found in private buildings as well as in public ones. One private mansion in Jerusalem extended to 600 square meters. Such buildings were decorated with rich frescoes and mosaics. It would have been hard for a rural tenant farmer not to have been impressed by the sheer grandeur of Hellenistic architecture. Some of this peasant wonder is caught by Mark 13:1: "Look, Teacher, what wonderful stones and what wonderful buildings!" Just as something of the prophetic rejection of such wealth and power is reflected in Jesus' reply: "Do you see these great buildings? There will not be left here one stone upon another, that will not be thrown down."

Galilean Cities

There were over thirty major cities in Palestine in the first century, each with its own history. Some were ancient cities reaching back into Old Testament times; others were recent foundations by the Herods. Some had a continuous history; others had been destroyed and subsequently rebuilt. In Galilee two cities were prominent: Sepphoris and Tiberias.

Sepphoris was situated just over the hill from Nazareth. References to it in Josephus occur first at the beginning of the first century B.C. (*Ant.* xiii.338). Under the Romans it was the administrative capital of Galilee, but was at the center of Jewish resistance after Herod's death in 4 B.C. (*Ant.* xvii.271). The Roman governor in Syria, Varus, had the city destroyed (4 B.C.) and the survivors sold into captivity (*Ant.* xvii.289). Subsequently under Herod Antipas the city was rebuilt and repopulated (*Ant.* xviii.27). It is not altogether clear what the ethnic composition of the city was. It remained loyal to the Romans during the Jewish War, though Josephus clearly implies that its population was Jewish (*War* iii.30–4). What is clear is that it was rebuilt as a major city of great architectural splendor and military strength. Again it is interesting to reflect on what impact all this might have made on Jesus. Stories of the destruction of Sepphoris must have abounded in Nazareth during Jesus' childhood, keeping alive his feelings of outrage, pride, and sorrow. At the same time the reconstruction of the city must have offered welcome employment and prosperity to local tradesmen.

Tiberias was a relatively late foundation (c. A.D. 26) by Herod Antipas that became his showpiece and capital (*Ant.* xviii.36–8). Its setting on Lake Gennesaret was geographically magnificent but religiously unfortunate. Building work exposed the remains of an ancient burial ground, which would have put it out of bounds to faithful Jews. Herod was therefore obliged to colonize it by force and the use of strong fiscal incentives. Its population was thus extremely mixed. Nevertheless, though deeply divided at the time of the Jewish War, the majority of the population came out against the Romans (Josephus, *Life* 32–42). The city eventually yielded to Vespasian, Nero's general subsequently to become emperor, and was spared (*War* iii.445–61). It contained a stadium and a synagogue of considerable splendor.

Jerusalem

The principal city in Palestine was of course Jerusalem, which was both like and unlike other cities. It was unlike other cities because it was the city of the Temple and the traditional center of the Jewish nation. Other aspects must have made it appear quite similar to other Hellenistic cities. For most Jews, Jerusalem was first and foremost where they came to worship at the major pilgrimages of Passover and Weeks and Tabernacles. This meant that it was a focus of Jewish unity, both for Jews in Palestine and for those living in other cities around the Mediterranean.

Traditionally Jerusalem was the center of Jewish power. God was King of the Jews and his presence resided in the Temple (Pss 76, 84, 99). The high priest represented the people to God and God to the people. As such he and the priesthood administered the Law and governed the people. If that was the theory, the practice was rather more complicated.

In the first place the high priest's authority was clearly dependent on the Roman authorities. He was appointed by the Roman governor, and a Roman garrison kept a watchful eye over the Temple courts. This permanent garrison was strengthened at the major feasts by reinforcements from Caesarea. Second, the high priest's authority was subject to the jurisdiction of the Sanhedrin. This was a court or council made up of priestly families and experts in the Law over which the high priest presided. Looked at through Roman eyes he was rather more like their appointee to the presidency of a city council, on the Greek model, than a divinely appointed ruler. Jews were divided: Most accepted him as the bearer of the traditional office of high priest, and some, like the Covenanters at Qumran, saw him as unacceptably compromised.

There were other respects, too, in which Jerusalem was more like a Greek city. In the first instance, the Temple was the basis of considerable wealth. Under Herod the Great a large program of rebuilding had begun that provided employment for many (*Ant.* xv.380–425). Pilgrims brought wealth to the city. Jews everywhere paid tax to the Temple; tithes were supposed to be brought to Jerusalem. Around the Temple there were a number of small industries. Jerusalem was the home of aristocratic families and wealthy landowners. All of this would create a sharp contrast between the wealthy city-dwellers and the poor from the land. Moreover the style and grandeur of the buildings in Jerusalem would underline the similarity with other Greek cities. Herod's Temple was Hellenistic in style.

Thus while Jerusalem had an enduring place in Jews' hearts

and affections, pilgrims to the city may often have felt a sense of estrangement. This will have rekindled old hopes for a New Jerusalem restored to its former purity and independence (e.g., Ez 40–7; Tb 14:5; 1 En 90:28; Mk 14:58; Test. Benj. 9:2).

Life in the Country

Most of Palestine of course lay outside the cities. Its population was predominantly Jewish and its economy agrarian. Its population lived in towns and villages, the latter being associated with their local town. The land was divided between large estates and small holdings.

Agriculture flourished during the time of Jesus and was the basis of a profitable export trade. Crops included wheat, barley, olives, rice, vegetables, flax, balsam, dates, and figs. Reading some contemporary accounts gives the impression of a generally prosperous community. On the other hand general prosperity depends on the equity of distribution of wealth and goods, more particularly on patterns of land tenure and on the availability of employment.

Patterns of land tenure were changing throughout this period. Under Herod I (37–4 B.C.) much of the land had been administered as the king's own estate. Subsequently his lands were sold off and this led to the increase of large estates often with absentee landlords (see Mt 21:33–41). Archaeological evidence shows the existence of such estates with a central settlement and dependent villages. These estates were in part sublet to tenant farmers paying rent either in kind or in cash. Labor on the estate proper was provided either by tenants or by day laborers (cf. Mt 20:1). Clearly under these circumstances the possibility of amassing debts and of shortage of employment was a real one, as the Gospels show (Mt 18:25; 20:6).

Again, prosperity can vary regionally. Much will depend on the suitability of the land for cultivation and on the pressure of population on the land. Two things suggest that conditions in Galilee away from the coastal strip were demanding. In the first place, Pompey's "liberation" of the coastal cities from the control of the Jews in the first century B.C. (*Ant.* xiv.75–6) probably impelled a sizeable population into the Galilean hinterland who then had to compete for land and work. Second, archaeological evidence shows that the land in the Galilean mountains was intensively farmed and parceled up into very small lots. The methods of farming were often very laborious: damming streams to stop the top soil running off, the use of a form of terracing, and so forth. All this indicates that farming was difficult and that pressure of population made it imperative to get as much from the land as possible.

Thus there are good grounds for supposing that life in rural Palestine was far from easy for peasant farmers and day laborers. Agriculture itself was laborious and the land, possibly the markets, and certainly wages were in the control of a few wealthy landowners. None of this makes for great security or an easy life. Debt, loss of tenancies, and ultimately slavery threatened. At the same time, rural workers would have been aware of the wealth and opportunities offered by the largely Hellenistic cities in their midst, and such prospects no doubt exercised a powerful attraction. Under these circumstances sustaining a traditional Jewish way of life required sustained effort.

Evidence of this can be found in three areas. First, there were considerable movements of population. We have already seen how new cities were built and populated during this period. Even where, as in the case of Tiberias, there were strong traditional reasons for not settling in a particular site, a mixture of financial incentives and coercion could succeed in establishing a community many of whose members ultimately showed a strong loyalty to the nation. People emigrated to join the many Jewish communities in cities round the Mediterranean, such as

Alexandria. These communities, as we have seen, were often numerically strong and contributed substantially to the wealth of Jerusalem (see *Ant.* xiv.110–18). Again a mixture of economic attraction and local pressures at home encouraged such movements. And a few Jews, deeply discontented with the conduct of the Temple and indeed of Jewish life in general, sought out a new way of life by removing to the desert community at Qumran.

Second, there were those who took to begging as the Gospels clearly show (Mk 10:46: Jn 9:8; Lk 14:21). Illness and physical disability meant that it was physically impossible for some to earn a living, and so they were left only with some form of recourse to public charity. The Gospels give ample evidence of the incidence of such illnesses and physical handicaps.

And there were, third, those who resorted to more violent ways of resolving their problems – thieves, brigands (Mt 6:19f.; 24:43; Lk 10:30), and resistance fighters, like those recorded, for example, in Josephus' account of the disturbances after Herod's death (*Ant.* xvii.206–23; 250–98). The two "thieves" crucified with Jesus were probably resistance fighters of this kind.

The Cultural Character of First-Century Palestine

The brief survey we have given of political, social, and economic factors in first-century Palestine shows how mixed a community it was. Precisely because it had been fought over for hundreds of years, it had been subjected to various kinds of cultural influence. In the next chapter we shall look at the Jewish cultural heritage. Here we must first consider briefly the character of the dominant alien culture that had infiltrated Palestine, namely, Hellenism.

One of the major turning points in the history of the Mediterranean world was the brief but brilliant career of Alexander the Great in the fourth century. The great Macedonian general swept through the Middle East and on into India, bequeathing to his generals an enormous empire. He also bequeathed to the territories he had conquered an international culture based on the Greek language.

Greek was already at that time an important language for purposes of trade. It now became the official language of the great empires Alexander's generals administered. Anyone who had aspirations to power within those territories had to learn Greek. This new culture had its institutions and monuments. Schools were set up that taught a syllabus based on Greek language and rhetoric, literature, drama and philosophy. Homer became part of the cultural heritage of the educated from Macedonia to Alexandria. Along with their education in language and literature, the young men who attended the schools also received training in physical skills, athletics, and gymnastics. Public contests were held in specially constructed stadia, which were thus a distinguishing feature of Hellenistic cities. So too were the temples to the Greek gods and goddesses, as well as the theaters in which performances of Greek plays were held.

Jewish reaction to such infiltration of foreign language, institutions, and religion was, predictably, mixed. Powerful families who wished to continue to hold positions of power and influence willingly seized the enhanced opportunities that were now offered if they joined the service of their foreign overlords (see the story of Joseph the Tobiad, *Ant.* xii.160–85). Other families on occasion became the focus of revolt. Greek became an accepted medium of Jewish culture and religion. The Scriptures were translated into Greek at Alexandria during the reign of Ptolemy Philadelphus (285–247 B.C., cf. Letter of Aristeas, paraphrased in *Ant.* xii.11–118). Jews in the cities, whether in Palestine or outside, would have spoken Greek. In time there would grow up a literature that would present Jewish customs and beliefs to the Greek world and command considerable respect. Notable among such writers from the first-century A.D. were the Jewish historian Josephus and the philosopher and theologian Philo at Alexandria.

At the same time Jews began to assimilate Greek ideas and institutions into their own culture. Jews took Greek names alongside their Hebrew or Aramaic names. Jewish ways of interpreting Scripture were probably influenced by Greek ways of interpreting Homer. Jewish schools were developed at the same time as the introduction of Greek schools. The Great Sanhedrin in Jerusalem, which is unknown in records before the time of Alexander, bears interesting resemblances to the councils of Greek cities. This is not to say that in all this Jews simply took over Greek forms. Rather the Jews adapted them significantly to their own cultural traditions and beliefs. Like any living culture Judaism adapted to the world in which it found itself.

It should be clear from even such a brief description that Hellenism was essentially an urban culture, even though wealthy Hellenists would often own large country estates. As we have already seen, Palestine contained many Hellenistic cities and these naturally became the centers of power both under Alexander's successors and then under the Romans. Thus the Hellenization of Palestine focused naturally on the control of the cities.

Control over the cities could change hands quite quickly. The Jewish Hasmonean dynasty established control over the coastal cities, but this passed to the Romans with the advent of Pompey's armies. The key question was of course control of Jerusalem. Under the Seleucids, the Syrian rulers who controlled Palestine in the third and beginning of the second century, Jerusalem became more and more like a Greek city. A gymnasium was built and young Jews took part in the games and even removed the mark of their circumcision to avoid popular derision (1 Mc 1:15; athletes competed naked). The high priest adopted a Greek name (*Ant.* xii.239–41) and Greek customs were widely accepted. The climax came, however, when the Syrian king attempted to destroy the Jewish religion itself and set up an altar to the Olympian Zeus in the Temple on top of the altar of burnt offerings (1 Mc 1:54–61). This led to the Maccabean revolt (166–140 B.C.) and the refounding of a Jewish monarchy. Yet while Jerusalem was thus delivered from the worst excesses of Hellenism, external pressures and influences did not simply go away. The rebuilding of the Temple under Herod I was undertaken in Hellenistic style. And if the Roman rulers did not dictate the nature of the Temple cult, at least they controlled the appointment of the high priest.

Summary

This chapter has conveyed something of the complexity of the political, social, economic, and cultural climate of first-century Palestine. In a word it was a country where control of power was uneasily balanced between the traditional families and institutions of Judaism and the Roman governor. This was reflected in the tension between the country areas and the towns, between those who spoke Greek and had adopted Greek ways and those who remained true to Jewish customs. It was a land where there were wide extremes of wealth and poverty. Those who had large land holdings or who were involved in international trade or politics had access to great wealth and power. Country peasants must often have struggled to survive. It was a country too where different cultural systems lived side by side, and where the pressures on the traditional ways of life were great. The attraction of the wealth and power associated with Hellenistic life and culture would have been great for those in a position to take advantage of it. The difficulties of making a living must have put different kinds of pressures on rural Jews who strove to be true to their traditions. We shall discuss the Jewish responses to this situation in more detail in the next chapter.

Chapter 2

Unity and Diversity in Judaism from the Third Century B.C.

Judaism in the first century was a diverse phenomenon. In the first place, many Jews lived outside Palestine and spoke Greek rather than Hebrew or Aramaic. Then, within Palestine itself there were different parties or schools of Judaism: Sadducees, Pharisees, Essenes, and Zealots, each of which had their own ideas about the proper form of Judaism. From time to time prophets would arise and stir up popular movements with great expectations. And there were the ordinary people who no doubt most of the time simply got along as best they could.

Others again must have found it difficult to remain true to their traditional way of life in any form. The options open to them varied considerably. At one end of the scale they could fall into various forms of destitution: slavery, begging, and brigandage. At the other end they could assimilate in one way or another to Hellenism. They might become officials, tax collectors, or courtiers of client kings who were effectively part of the international community of the Mediterranean. Less grandly they might move into the Hellenistic cities and seek to pursue their way of life there as best they could. Not all such Jews would by any means have seen themselves as abandoning the ways of their fathers.

Despite this great diversity, the various forms of Jewish life were all recognizably Jewish. They represent, that is to say, different ways of working out a certain core of beliefs and practices that was widely accepted as fundamental to Judaism.

Such diversity had not grown up overnight, nor was it without its roots in the troubled history of the Jews. It goes back at least as far as the third century and is the product of Jews' attempts to work out the best way to respond to the pressures that foreign domination and the proximity of a powerful alien culture put on their traditional way of life. In this chapter we shall attempt to trace something of the history of Jewish responses to such pressures so as to set the scene for a more detailed study of the main Jewish groups in the first century.

The Basic Beliefs of Ancient Judaism

The diversity in the Judaism of this period was, I would suggest, rooted in a central core of beliefs and practices. Of course it is not only such beliefs and practices that hold groups together. Accidents of history, language, and geography all constitute important markers of a group's identity. But some common pattern of beliefs and practices is necessary if a group is to have any meaningful sense of identity that will enable it to hold together under strain. The practice of certain forms of democracy, belief in certain notions of "fair play," tolerance, and human freedom undoubtedly helped to stiffen national resolve among the Western Allies during the Second World War, and also formed a barrier to the development of harmonious relations with the Soviet Union after the war. Belief in and the enforcement of apartheid has effectively held together the white population of South Africa for the last few decades. With its official abandonment and yet continued practice, white South Africans are faced with a deep crisis of identity that threatens to fragment their society.

Such basic beliefs and practices, like the belief in freedom, can of course take many forms. They are rather like the text of a play, which can be performed in many ways. Some performances are controversial and may even lead people to deny that they are true performances at all. But in an obvious sense they are all still performances of the same text.

What then were the basic beliefs and practices of Jews in the first century? First and foremost they believed they had been chosen by God and that God had made an agreement with them by which they were bound to him and he to them. "Now therefore, if you will obey my voice and keep my covenant, you shall be my own possession among all peoples; for all the earth is mine, and you shall be to me a kingdom of priests and a holy nation" (Ex 19:5–6). This was a gracious relationship dependent on God's mercy. "You have seen what I did to the Egyptians and how I bore you on eagles' wings and brought you to myself" (ibid. v.4). But, though there was no question of the Jews' having earned such favors, the continuance of this relationship was subject to conditions. God had made an agreement, a covenant, with the people. If they obeyed his Law, he would bless them. This blessing was specifically connected with the promise of a land flowing with milk and honey (Dt 6:1–3). It is this promise that holds together the different calls and promises made to the founding figures of the nation: "The land which he swore to your fathers, to Abraham, to Isaac, and to Jacob, to give you" (Dt 6:10). Thus belief in election, covenant, the observance of the Law, and the promise of the land were the cornerstones of Judaism.

There were other beliefs too that were accepted unquestioningly. Jews believed that there was only one God (Dt 6:4) and that he was the creator of the world and sovereign over all the powers of evil. They believed that the terms of the Covenant were set out in Scripture, more particularly in the first five books of the Scriptures, which constituted the Law. The Jewish Scriptures were believed to be divinely inspired. The practices and institutions they prescribed – circumcision, the Temple, the priesthood – were believed to be divinely ordained.

It seems most likely that most Jews of the period would have readily subscribed to most if not all of these practices and beliefs. Other beliefs were more controversial. To what extent did God reward the righteous here on earth? To what extent were Jewish election and the Covenant tied to some notion, not only of the land, but of a Jewish monarchy modeled after David's kingdom? What was the place of the other nations in God's plan? These were all matters where Jewish history and individual experience might raise difficult questions. Wrestling with such questions might produce much debate and eventually a body of literature that addressed these issues.

There should be nothing very surprising in this. In any community there are certain practices and beliefs that are taken more or less for granted. They are the sort of beliefs that people appeal to in order to clinch an argument or which they simply assume when arguing. They are in fact the kinds of beliefs that make interesting arguments possible. The arguments, as it were, stem from the conflicts that arise when we start asking for greater clarification of some of these beliefs.

The same is true in Judaism. God has chosen the Jews, but what does that say about the Gentiles? Are they therefore lost forever (Lv 20:22–6)? Or will God one day bring them into the circle of his grace through the Jews (Is 60:1–3)? May they sometimes indeed be instruments of God to punish his people (Hb 1:6; Jer 20:1–6)? If the Gentiles oppress Jews, occupy their land, and subvert their customs, then what? Circumcision may be the mark of a man's entry into the Covenant (Gn 17:9–14), but is it a sufficient sign of the Covenant relationship? What if those who are circumcised are faithless? May not some further rite be required? John the Baptist's water baptism and the oath that the members of the community at Qumran had to swear on entry can be seen as attempts to answer this. Jewish practice and theology can be seen as the attempt to work out the meaning of such basic beliefs, as they are tested by experience. Such theology, particularly if it is subsequently enshrined in sacred texts, then becomes part of the equipment of a people as it continues to grapple with the tensions between its experience and its basic beliefs.

Grounds for Questioning

Where then in practice did the tensions come? Jews believed that God had chosen them, that he had promised to be their God and to give them the land if they obeyed his Covenant. Yet their land was constantly under the domination of foreign powers who invaded their territory and subverted their rulers. Had Israel failed? Had God reneged on his promises? Was the final reckoning still to come?

One can see these concerns surfacing in the Wisdom literature that was still being actively developed in the third and second centuries. Books like Qoheleth (Ecclesiastes) and Sirach (Ecclesiasticus) grappled (as Job and Wisdom had done before) with the belief that God would reward the righteous and punish the wicked. There was of course nothing particularly Jewish about such a belief. Anyone who believes that God is just and that justice is properly administered through a system of rewards and punishments will hold such a belief. The problem for Jewish writers lay specifically in what was meant by "the righteous" and "the wicked." Leaving aside the question of how far there might be knowledge of God's will outside Israel, it was axiomatic for them that it was in the Law that God's will had been most clearly revealed. Thus those who obeyed the Law were most clearly righteous and those who disobeyed it were most obviously wicked. Yet as Hellenistic forms of administration and commerce extended over Palestine it was inevitable that material rewards – wealth, power, and influence – should go principally to those who became "Hellenized," to those who lived in the cities or who attached themselves to the courts of the rulers. Yet those who became Hellenized would be tempted to be faithless to many of the prescriptions of the Law, in the end to ally themselves to those who wished to proscribe it (1 Mc 1:41–3). Why then did the obviously wicked prosper and the obviously righteous suffer?

Such questions had troubled the writer of Psalm 73: "For I was envious of the arrogant, when I saw the prosperity of the wicked" (v. 3). The people clearly are drawn to such material prosperity and disdain God: "And they say, 'How can God know? Is there knowledge in the Most High?'", while the righteous man suffers: "For all the day long have I been stricken, and chastened every morning" (vv. 11, 14). Nevertheless he derives comfort from the worship of the sanctuary and holds fast to his belief that in the end God will reward the wicked appropriately. "For lo, those who are far from thee shall perish; thou dost put an end to those who are false to thee. But for me it is good to be near God" (vv. 27–8).

There is here a real conflict between Jews' belief and their historic experience that would have been keenly felt in the third and second centuries. But it is important to see that this conflict comes not between the fact that the wicked were prospering and the bare belief that God would bless the righteous. The conflict is between the prosperity of the wicked and a belief that God will bless the righteous *in this world with material blessings.*

The problem was that such present material blessing of the righteous might be more or less assured in an independent Jewish state with Jewish laws and courts. However, once Hellenistic institutions and offices became intermixed with and even superimposed on Jewish ones, then such assurance could no longer be given. Thus the question for Jews might be either a theoretical one or a practical one: How can we make sense of God's righteousness, his purposes, when the wicked prosper? Or, how or when will the wicked be ousted so that Israel can once again possess the land for its own? Needless to say these two trains of questioning are often closely intertwined.

There is another point of no small importance. How sharply people perceive such conflicts between their beliefs and experience will vary considerably. The writer of Ecclesiastes strikes one as a person of keen sensibility. He saw deep contradictions within Jewish society where others went on hoping that all would come right in the end. He comes close to denying that there is any rationale to be discerned in God's dealings with the world: "That which is, is far off, and deep, very deep; who can find it out?" (7:24). Thus while holding fast to his belief in God's righteousness (3:16–17), he effectively discards belief in the just apportionment of rewards and punishments in this life: "In my vain life I have seen everything; there is a righteous man who perishes in his righteousness, and there is a wicked man who prolongs his life in his evil-doing" (7:15).

For others the tensions were there but could probably be met with a little adjustment, a little lowering of one's sights and rather more ignoring of the unacceptable. The writer of Ecclesiasticus, a work included in the Apocrypha, certainly sees things more superficially than the canonical preacher of the book of Ecclesiastes. Sirach reaffirms the possibility of wisdom: "All wisdom is the fear of the Lord, and in all wisdom there is the fulfillment of the Law" (Sir 19:20). But while he reaffirms the link between righteousness and God's governance of the world, when it comes to the question of rewards in this world he resorts to the past, praising the works of the forefathers who were duly rewarded (Ecclus 44). In this respect he is a fairly typical reactionary, reaffirming past beliefs and glories at a time when they were in fact being seriously challenged, freely issuing criticism and advice to the Jewish aristocracy, while failing to grasp the political realities that were undermining the kind of Judaism he espoused.

But when, under Antiochus Epiphanes, Judaism was officially proscribed and punishable by death, such conflicts could no longer be ignored, even by the most optimistic. Such moments of crisis may lead to the reformulation of a group's beliefs and expectations in a quite radical way. The belief in present material rewards for the righteous may be abandoned altogether. Belief in a coming resurrection, in the ushering in of a new world when all will be resolved, stirs (Dn 12:2). Yet all this may still occur within the framework of those very basic beliefs that I have suggested were held by most Jews most of the time.

Some Developments in Judaism Arising out of the Maccabean Revolt

We should now look in a little more detail at some of the movements in Jewish thought and practice in the two centuries before Jesus' day. Let us recall the situation at the beginning of the second century. The Seleucids in Syria were overlords of Palestine. Jerusalem and the high priests were embracing Hellenism with considerable enthusiasm. Young Jews who wished to become Hellenized were even undergoing painful operations to remove the marks of their circumcision (1 Mc 1:10–15). But the Seleucid ruler Antiochus Epiphanes was not satisfied even with this measure of cultural adaptation. He attempted to proscribe the observance of Judaism altogether and finally had an altar erected to Zeus in the Temple (1 Mc 1:54–64).

Jewish reactions to this situation were complex. Some are described in the first book of Maccabees. The first chapter records the faithlessness of many Jews. Not only did they support the earlier reforms and introduction of Hellenistic institutions but they were ready to comply with the new laws enforcing pagan sacrifice (1 Mc 1:41–53; cf. *Ant.* xii.248–56 with greater emphasis on the widespread Jewish resistance). This widespread faithlessness is contrasted with the attitudes and behavior of Mattathias and his sons. Mattathias was a member of a leading Jewish family who moved from Jerusalem to Modein during this period. Here he was urged by Antiochus' officials to sacrifice on the pagan altar. In return he and his sons would be rewarded and become the king's friends. Instead of complying, Mattathias, "burning with zeal," attacked a Jew who was sacrificing on the altar and killed him and the king's official. He and his sons then fled to the hills, "leaving all that they had" (1 Mc 2:1–28).

This marks the beginning of the Maccabean revolt, named after Mattathias' son, Judas Maccabeus. The ultimate success of the revolt was dependent not a little on the complex politics of the Middle East. Nevertheless Maccabean "zeal for the law" played an important part in sustaining the Jewish revolt. The story of the Maccabees, remembered yearly at the festival of Hannukah, remained with Jews as an image of steadfast loyalty to the traditions of Israel.

Two aspects of the story of Mattathias are worth noting in particular. The first is the comparison the author draws between Mattathias and Phinehas, the grandson of Aaron, Moses' priest: "Thus he burned with zeal for the law, as Phinehas did against Zimri the son of Salu" (1 Mc 2:26). The story of Phinehas and Zimri in Numbers 25 is set at a time when the people of Israel have been sacrificing to Baal and are being severely punished by Moses and God for it. Zimri has the mistaken temerity to choose this as a time to bring a Midianite woman into the camp. Phinehas follows them to Zimri's tent and spears the two of them as they lie together. This act of inspired vengeance – which is strictly a breach of the legal procedures – is compared with God's zeal. "He was zealous with my zeal among them, so that I did not consume the people of Israel in my zeal" (Nm 25:11). And this is sealed by a covenant of peace between Phinehas and his descendants and God that bestows on them an eternal priesthood. Just as the penalties for breach of such avoidance rules are severe, so too the rewards for compliance are great: permanent membership in the central cadres of the nation. Thus it is a story that inculcates the abomination both of sacrificing to idols and of going with foreign women. To be zealous for the Law is to abstain from all contact with foreign ways and women. In the context of the Maccabean revolt such a story would clearly have helped to stiffen military resistance to the Hellenistic rulers who threatened Israel's traditions.

It compares interestingly with the story Josephus tells about Joseph the Tobiad, who lived a century before the Maccabees (*Ant.* xii.186–9). Joseph, a Hellenizing Jew, falls in love with a local dancer while on a visit to Alexandria. Knowing that intercourse with foreigners was prohibited, he enlists his brother's help in concealing his intended relationship. His brother, however, substitutes his own daughter for the dancer. Joseph, so drunk that he does not even notice the switch, becomes inflamed by her and eventually agrees to marry her. This grim little story, which says much to us about the treatment of women in ancient society, was of course intended to emphasize the importance, even for Hellenized or assimilating Jews, of remaining faithful to the traditions, of staying within the group's prescribed boundaries.

The other point about the story of the Maccabees' revolt is to notice the term in which Mattathias explains his refusal to sacrifice. Even if other nations are faithless to the traditions of their forebears, he will be faithful to the traditions of his. "I and my sons and my brothers will live by the covenant of our fathers" (1 Mc 2:20). This argument would have been well understood in the Hellenistic world. Respect for traditions was a primary virtue. Antiochus was offending against a general principle reaching back to Alexander that peoples should be allowed to live in accordance with the traditions of their fathers. Thus – in the story at least – Mattathias justifies his stance against Antiochus by appeal to a Hellenistic argument. The reference to the "covenant," however, gives it a specifically Jewish turn.

Mattathias' response to the crisis caused by Antiochus Epiphanes was not the only one. In the Book of Daniel we have a more visionary response. Written during the period of Seleucid oppression, it encourages Israel to hope for an act of divine intervention that will restore justice to the suffering saints.

Daniel is a strange work and is not easy to decode. The first part of the book tells the story of a young Jewish noble during the Babylonian exile who serves under various Babylonian kings – Nebuchadnezzar, Belshazzar, Darius, and Cyrus. Far from simply assimilating to Babylonian ways, Daniel stead-fastly refuses to defile himself with the king's food or to aban-don the beliefs of his fathers, even though this leads to his ordeal in the lions' den (Dn 6). Instead he brings God's judg-ment to Nebuchadnezzar and Belshazzar by his interpretations of dreams – both the kings' and his own. When Belshazzar makes a great feast and brings in the Temple vessels, it is Daniel who interprets the "writing on the wall" as portending God's judgment on the king's desecration of the holy vessels (Dn 5). It is God who strikes down the king in the night. Thus Daniel, at least in the first six chapters, is the type of faithful Jewish official who enters foreign government service but re-fuses to abandon the ways of his fathers. In this he prospers and under Darius becomes a powerful ruler. In this respect, the first part of the book carries a message not so very different from that of the story about Joseph the Tobiad. The latter chapters of the book seem, however, to reflect a darker view of things. From Chapter 7 onward a new series of visions, this time Daniel's own, is recorded and we are taken back again into the reign of Belshazzar. In Chapter 7 Daniel dreams of four beasts, each more fearsome than the last. These visions then give way to a vision of the courtroom of heaven and the destruction of the fourth beast. Finally a figure like a (son of) man is presented to God and given power over all. The interpretation of the vision is relatively clear. The four beasts stand for the king-doms of the world, the fourth of which has sorely oppressed

Israel. The figure with a human face stands for the saints of the Most High who will reign when the beast has been overthrown by God. In the end Israel will triumph.

But only in the end. The picture is darker. The saints will be tried and tested and the suffering will be great. Such suffering, as is explained later in the book, is the result of Israel's faithlessness to the Covenant (Daniel's prayer, 9:3–19). Indeed, the suffering is so great that Daniel's visions become more and more concerned with the question of when the end will come. A series of figures appear to him who reveal the pattern of the events at the end of time. Many of the explanations can reasonably be linked to events at the time of Antiochus. But in the end Daniel looks forward to a divine intervention when the archangel Michael will come and, after a time of great turmoil, deliver the faithful. Then the dead shall awake, "some to everlasting life, and some to shame and everlasting contempt" (12:2).

The later chapters of Daniel, written as they were at the height of the Hellenistic crisis under the Seleucids, mark an important shift in Jewish thinking. The severity of the attack on the Jewish way of life and the suffering of faithful Jews were so great (see the vivid description in *Ant.* xii.248–56) that they could no longer cling to the former belief that God would reward the faithful in this life. For the writer-seer the righteous are, above all, those who suffer because of their faithfulness and whose reward will come only after a prolonged period of testing in which many will perish. Thus only if the dead awake can justice be done: the righteous rewarded and the wicked punished. Such disasters have not, according to Daniel, fallen on Israel unmerited. They are due to Israel's lack of zeal for the Law, and Israel must respond by greater faithfulness to the Law. In return God will ultimately act to vindicate them. Thus on the one hand Daniel leaves everything to God, believing that he will finally act to save Israel. On the other hand Daniel demands total obedience to the Law and the Covenant, believing that it is the Jews' unfaithfulness that has brought trouble upon them.

Thus in this period we see the emergence of two rather different responses to cultural and political threats. One urges vigorous resistance to foreign infiltration, while the other pleads for a renewal of allegiance to the Law and looks for a new world in which all will receive their due deserts.

In these basic reactions lies the seed of much that was to come. Theoretically, these two concerns were wholly compatible with each other. If Israel kept the Law, God would guarantee its independence. Practically, however, there were tensions. The Jewish state could survive only if its leaders were prepared to enter into some form of compromise with the surrounding powers. To govern effectively, Jewish – or indeed Roman – rulers needed to control Jewish sacred institutions, which under the Law were seen as divinely appointed. The price of independence was the dovetailing of Jewish institutions into the Hellenistic world. Often this could be done without conflict; on occasion blatant or sustained interference would lead to resistance.

And if those who primarily sought Jewish political independence had to compromise, so too had those whose primary concern was the fulfillment of the Law. Apart from anything else the Pentateuch (the first five books of our Bible) contained a vast amount of legal material. Moreover, much of it was originally designed for very different – nomadic and pastoral – conditions from those of Palestine in the first centuries B.C. and A.D. Some of it was confusing or contradictory. The rules about tithing required careful interpretation to make any sense of them at all. More important, life for much of the rural population was so arduous that simply finding time and energy to give to more detailed matters of the Law would have been difficult. Some measure of adjustment to difficult conditions was inevitable.

The Aftermath: Developments in the Jewish Renewal Movement

National crises may set lines for subsequent developments. New expressions of basic beliefs are given that mean that those beliefs are never quite the same again. The return to a measure of normality, however, provides a different setting for the working out of new beliefs forged in crisis.

When in 140 B.C. the Maccabean revolt eventually led to the establishment of a Jewish dynasty, many no doubt saw this as the great opportunity for national renewal. But those whose aims had been principally the restoration of national sovereignty then had to face up to the realities of holding on to power in a hostile and dangerous world. Even their success in gaining power had been heavily dependent on the support of their neighbors. To remain in power they had to play the game of international politics skillfully and with resolve. This meant embracing Hellenism, for that was the currency of international affairs.

The dynasties that ruled the Jewish nation for the next two hundred years, the Hasmoneans and the Herods, paid their tribute to the Hellenistic world in full, as we have already seen. This led to considerable territorial expansion, not least to the repossession of Galilee by John Hyrcanus, high priest and ethnarch, at the end of the second century B.C. It also meant that Jewish rulers became more and more dependent for their military and political power on alliances with other states. The culmination of this tendency was Herod the Great's rapid change of sides from Mark Anthony to Octavian, later Augustus, during the Roman civil war. This may have ensured Herod's position as king; it also emphasized his position as a Roman puppet who could at will be deposed and his territory incorporated into the system of Roman provincial administration. Full political independence in a world of great superpowers is a dream for the enthusiasts. Those who have to exercise power know there is a price to be paid for even a measure of freedom to control one's own affairs.

This does not mean that there were not plenty of Jews who dreamed dreams or who were simply unhappy to pay the price of subservience to more powerful states, a price that fell more heavily on some than on others. There were many who saw the victory of the Maccabees as a great opportunity for the renewal of Jewish customs and faithfulness to the Law. It was after all zeal for the Law that had inspired the revolt. 1 Maccabees 2:42 tells of the party of the Hasideans, the pious or godly ones, who had played a major part in raising support for the revolt. Where they came from we do not know, but many scholars trace the beginnings of the emerging Jewish parties back to them. To the more enthusiastic members of this group Hasmonean diplomacy and compromise would have seemed a rank betrayal of all that had been fought for. It is probably among such that we should look for the founders of the community at the Dead Sea, the Essenes.

Much light has been cast on the history of this group by the discovery of their library hidden in the hills above the Dead Sea in the late 1940s and early 1950s. They rejected the ways of the Jewish ruler whom they labeled the Wicked Priest (1QpHab 8.9–13.4). This most likely refers to Jonathan Maccabee, who was made high priest by Alexander Balas, the Seleucid ruler, in 152 B.C. The community established a base on the shores of the Dead Sea where they lived, sharing their property and being instructed in the true understanding of the Law by their leader, the Teacher of Righteousness, who emerged some twenty years after the desecration of the Temple by Antiochus Epiphanes (CD 1.1–2.1). Here they sought to prepare the way of the Lord, looking for an act of divine intervention to establish total Jewish independence and sovereignty. In the end the nearest they got to it was in the life of their own isolated community. It was a preparation for the final age and in some ways an anticipation of it.

Other Jews, while regretting some of the compromises that subsequent Jewish rulers made, may still have seen the achievement of national independence as a great opportunity to implement the Law on a national basis. The complex history of the Pharisees has its genesis here. It starts as a court-based movement of national renewal. The mistakes of the past must be avoided. Israel must never again incur the wrath of God by its faithlessness. Yet proper implementation of the Law would require careful interpretation of its written prescriptions. The Pharisees believed there was an oral tradition, also divinely inspired and given to Moses, that could help them perform this important task (*Ant.* xiii.297). Thus they set about building a body of case law that would make it possible to have a national system of laws applicable to the conditions of their age.

Such aspirations to control national life can hardly have commended themselves to the Hasmoneans. They too were vigorously seeking such control, not least by usurping the high priesthood. The predictable clash came first under John Hyrcanus (134–104 B.C.) and then more fiercely under Alexander Jannaeus (103–76; *Ant.* xiii.288–98, 376). It is possible that at that point many Pharisees went off to Qumran to join the Essenes. Later under Alexandra (76–67) the Pharisees, who all along had enjoyed the support of the masses, were restored to favor (*Ant.* xiii.408–18).

The story of the Pharisees' clash with John Hyrcanus is interesting. The conflict was sparked by a suggestion made by a Pharisee at a feast given by the prince that John should renounce the high priesthood because his mother had been a captive in the reign of Antiochus Epiphanes. The complication was clearly that his mother had been raped and defiled, thereby disqualifying her son from the high priesthood (cf. Lv 21:14). Again the point is about intermixing, which reflects clearly enough the real issue: the continuing links of the Hasmonean rulers with foreign powers.

However that may be, the long period of estrangement from

the rulers marked the beginning of a transition within Pharisaism from the court at Jerusalem to the courts and synagogues in towns and villages. In the long run this would lead to the development of a religion whose base was predominantly the home and the family.

The Pharisees were not of course the only people who sought to maintain a position in Jerusalem. As a movement of scribes, or wise men, they had to dispute their place with the priestly aristocracy, the Sadducees. This party, as the name suggests, claimed descent from Zadok the priest and thus saw themselves to be in a continuous line with those who had, at least since the Restoration after the Exile, maintained the Temple cult in Jerusalem. As priests they clearly would have regarded the maintenance of the Temple cult as fundamental to the survival of Israel and to the maintenance of its relation to God. As members of an aristocracy who had been put in place after the Exile by the Persian king, they were familiar with owing their position and status to foreign rulers. By all accounts they were pragmatists, not popular with the people, not anxious to embrace radical solutions to Israel's predicament. As traditionalists they sought to retain what – to them at least – was best in the nation's heritage and that included its rich history of liturgical worship and their own inherited roles within it.

Conclusion

It is interesting to consider how these emerging groups, the Essenes, the Pharisees, and the Saduccees, relate to the developments in Judaism that took place at the time of the Maccabean revolt. At that point there arose, we have said, on the one hand a vigorous national resistance movement that would fight to restore national sovereignty and, on the other, the vision of a new world to be created by divine or angelic intervention whereby an end would be put to present suffering. These are both readily intelligible responses to the terrible events of Antiochus Epiphanes' reign, and though they are practically and theoretically quite different they are both rooted in zeal for the Law and the traditions of the nation.

The problems arise of course when the revolution succeeds and the new age dawns and the opportunity is given to put the program into effect. In the first instance, for the resistance fighters, access to power does not mean untrammeled sovereignty and freedom of action. On the contrary, they have to learn to compromise in order to maintain such independence as they have. In this sense they will be pushed more toward the Sadducean party, the old priestly aristocracy who had been in the business of accommodating to foreign powers since at least the time of the Ptolemies. So long as certain institutions were maintained, the Temple and the dynasty, much else might be sacrificed, at least temporarily. It was a dangerous path, for were not the perils of accommodating to foreign powers exactly what the Maccabees had originally revolted against? And might they not eventually find themselves the target of movements who took their inspiration from their own founding fathers?

On the other hand, if a measure of independence had been achieved, then was not this to be seen as a major opportunity to restore Israel's traditions, to renew the life of the nation as a counterculture in the predominantly Hellenistic Mediterranean? It is interesting here to note the popularity of the Pharisees at this time. The mass of the people supported them – the mass, that is, of those who derived little direct benefit from the world of international commerce and politics. But the Pharisees' position was a difficult one too. Their zeal for Jewish tradition inevitably brought them into conflict with rulers who had to pursue systematically a policy of interacting with the surrounding Hellenistic world. They could not, in the long run, enjoy a base at court. And so they were gradually forced to retreat from the central political scene and to seek a base in the local communities.

But what of the continuing attraction of dreams of a new age? As we have seen, some decided early that what they had hoped for had not been realized and so took themselves off to await the end from a base outside, or at least as far as possible outside, the confines of Jewish society. The reasons for this disappointment were complex. Exclusion from power in the new regime would certainly have played its part, not least in terms of disputes about who were the rightful heirs to the high priesthood.

Others may have been prepared to await events and to keep alive the hope of some more radical change in Israel's fortunes. That is to say, such hopes would have simmered on, always ready to be revived when events took a turn for the worse, when the chances of achieving true independence and sovereignty, prosperity and well-being seemed, once again, cruelly dashed. It is perhaps then understandable that as the Roman grip on Palestine grew, movements inspired by such hopes for the future would again make their appearance.

Chapter 3

Membership of the People of God

We have been considering the ways in which prolonged exposure to foreign rule and influence made it difficult for Jews to maintain their traditional way of life, undermined their sovereignty and national identity, made them long for some resolution to their problems, and on occasion brought them into direct and costly conflict with their foreign overlords.

When groups are under threat from alien forces as were the Jews it is natural for them to begin to ask questions about their own identity, about what it is to be a Jew, what it is to be a member of the group. In the first place there is an obvious sense in which people in situations of crisis and conflict want to know not merely who belongs to their group but whose loyalty can be counted on in the struggle against the foe. In France during World War Two it would not have been enough to know that someone was French. One would have had to ask was she a true Frenchwoman? The answers to such a question would have varied, moreover, in accordance with the views that were taken of where the national interest lay. That is to say, under such circumstances, it would not have been enough to appeal to standard definitions of group membership: birth, nationality, education, language. Further marks of membership would be required, for example, membership of or support for certain subgroups, such as the Resistance, and the espousal of certain policies.

The period of Roman dominance over Palestine provided enough crisis points at which such questions of group loyalty were raised: the disturbances at the time of Herod's death that saw the emergence of Judas the Galilean, the revolt at the time of the census under Quirinius, and of course the Jewish war that led to the destruction of Jerusalem in A.D. 70. But even in the periods of relative quiet under Tiberius, questions of loyalty were raised by the very existence of collaborators with the Romans: client rulers, members of cities who had received their freedom from Rome, tax collectors and minor officials.

Questions about group identity may not, however, be concerned simply with questions of group loyalty: Who is a true Jew? Prolonged exposure to foreign influence undermines a people's sense of its own self-respect and identity. The question may be rather: What is it to be a Jew? How do I recover a sense of pride in being Jewish? One of the marks of cultural oppression is that the dominant group seeks to impose its own definitions on the subordinate group. This is what has happened in South Africa, where the white minority has attempted to inculcate into the black population its own low estimate of their worth. This is achieved through providing different and inferior forms of education, through legislation that underlines the inferior status of blacks at different points of social and political life, more widely through the development of linguistic terms and associations that convey a low view of blacks. Movements like Steve Biko's Black Consciousness Movement are then attempts to reassert black people's own sense of their worth and specific identity, to discard the low self-image that has been imposed on them. Similarly, Roman control of Jewish institutions and offices like the monarchy and the high priesthood together with the economic and cultural dominance of Greek cities and education no doubt suggested to Jews themselves the inferiority of their own social, political, and cultural institutions. And this in turn led to a reaction, to attempts to reaffirm the importance of the Jewish tradition.

Certainly such questions of the nature of group membership and loyalty were actively canvassed by Jews at the time of

Jesus. Given the basic framework of belief in election and the Covenant we can expect broad agreement on certain matters of belief and practice. Nevertheless, on points of interpretation and implementation we may expect to find more detailed disagreement.

One way of thinking about what the standard idea of Jewishness in the first century was is to try and compile a list of what Jews of the time would have regarded as essential for Jewishness. Such a list might include: birth to a Jewish mother or father; circumcision; observance of dietary laws; observance of certain days and feasts – Sabbath, Passover, the Day of Atonement; belief in the inspiration of Jewish Scripture; belief in one God; belief in the Covenant; belief in Torah; visits to the Temple; tithing; paying Temple tax.

Probably most first-century Jews in Galilee regarded most of these points as important. But we are at least aware of Jews in the immediately preceding period who had so far assimilated to Hellenism that they actually attempted to conceal the marks of their circumcision (1 Mc 1:15). Did they cease to think of themselves as Jews *at all?* Or did they think of themselves as enlightened, reformed Jews? Possibly the latter, particularly if they aspired after leadership of the Jewish people. Such examples are extreme, but it is nevertheless likely that they mark the far end of a broad spectrum of a variety of practices among those who thought of themselves as Jews. Most Jews regarded Jewish descent and circumcision, the observance of food laws and the Sabbath as essential. There was perhaps more fluctuation about tithing and visits to Jerusalem, but the presence of large crowds at the major festivals, some of whom had traveled considerable distances to get there, shows that here too there was still strong popular support.

All this, however, is to do no more than list certain distinguishing features of Judaism to which most Jews who sought to uphold Jewishness would have subscribed. Such people would clearly have seen themselves first and foremost *as Jews*. Others, doubtless a minority, may have regarded their membership of the Greek-speaking world of international trade, diplomacy, and culture as equally or indeed as more important. They may, therefore, have been prepared to abandon or reinterpret certain features of Judaism where necessary. Our interest here, however, is in those groups that actively sought to promote a greater sense of Jewish identity and loyalty. In this we shall have to consider both the Jewish renewal groups like the Zealots, the Pharisees, and the Essenes, who like the earlier Hasidaeans (1 Mc 2:42) "offered themselves willingly for the Law," but also others like the Sadducees and the high priests who were more interested in seeing themselves, not as Jews simpliciter, but as Jews with a definable position within the world of the Roman principate. For all these groups we shall need to consider how their specific emphases related to commonly accepted ideas of Jewishness of the time.

For most Jews descent from Jewish parents would have been the basis of their Jewishness. And for male Jews circumcision would have been a further necessary condition. Descent, witness the genealogies in the New Testament (Mt 1:1–17; Lk 3:23–38), was through the male line. Jewish society was organized into tribes and families. Family membership was an important means of determining status. Priests and Levites held their offices by virtue of descent. Certain powerful families, like the Hasmoneans, the Herods, and the family of Judas the Galilean (*Ant.* xvii.271), wielded great political influence.

In this respect Jewish society was like many other societies. What was of particular significance was that it traced its origins back to the patriarchs, above all to Abraham. It was to Abraham that the promise was given: the promise that he would be the father of a great nation and that his descendants would inherit the land. The sign of this covenant was circumcision. Every male of Abraham's household was to be circumcised at eight days, whether he was Abraham's offspring or whether he was bought from foreigners. Those who were circumcised were heirs of the promises; those who were not were to be cut off from the people (Gn 15–17).

The story of Abraham's faith and the promises made to him by God is of course a rich one, and the Genesis accounts already doubtless represent the result of much telling and retelling. Subsequent generations would repeat the process: Abraham's faith in the face of the appalling test to which God subjected him (Gn 22) was one element in the drama. God's promise of the election of Israel sealed by the sign of circumcision was another. But who were Abraham's true descendants? Those who were circumcised? Those who were physically descended from Abraham? Those who had faith in the promises? For most Jews, descent and circumcision went easily enough together. Genesis 17 certainly allowed for the admission of those of non-Jewish descent even if subsequent Jewish proselytes were not bought from foreigners. But proselytes in Palestine were probably rare. Thus for most Jews, being born of Jewish parents and, in the case of males, being circumcised were the basis of membership of the people whom God had chosen and to whom he had given the Law and the land.

But while that was no doubt widely understood and accepted, it did not mean there were no disputes, even among the Jewish renewal groups. Of course what we have in our records are probably rather specialized debates. They represent less the opinions of the broad generality of people than those of people particularly aware of the conflicts between Jewish beliefs and experience.

It is not difficult to imagine how such conflicts might arise. Jews believed that God had promised Abraham's descendants that they would inherit the land. As a sign of this they were to be circumcised. But while they had indeed inherited the land it was now occupied by alien forces. Why? Was God not faithful to his promises? Or were descent and circumcision of themselves not enough? The simple answer to this – echoing Daniel 9 – is that, additionally, Jews were required to observe the Law given to Moses and that it was their failure to do this that had led to their downfall.

Certainly in the two centuries before the Christian era there is evidence of such questions being discussed in some detail. An interesting example is in Jubilees, a book dating back probably to the second century B.C. and foreshadowing some of the ideas to be found in the Qumran writings. There, after retelling the story of Genesis 17, the writer adds his own commentary. He first emphasizes the eternal validity of the commandment of circumcision: "And anyone who is born whose own flesh is not circumcised on the eighth day is not from the sons of the covenant which the Lord made for Abraham since (he is) from the children of destruction" (Jub. 15.26). Doubtless the attempts by some Jews to remove the marks of circumcision may have prompted some of the fierceness of this affirmation (cf. too the Mishnah, m.Aboth 3.12). Circumcision is the seal of salvation. Those who have no such sign upon them will be destroyed (Jub. 15.26) for God has made a radical distinction between the people of the Covenant and all others. Over the nations he has caused spirits to rule to lead them astray. No such spirit rules over Israel, for God alone is their ruler (Jub. 15.32). And this contrasts neatly with another text from the same period: Sirach 44:19–21. It too connects the Covenant with Abraham's circumcision: "He established the covenant in his flesh" (v. 20), but goes on to assert that this would be a blessing for the nations (v. 21), even if the blessing seems likely to come in the form of some universal Jewish rule: Abraham's descendants will "inherit from the River to the ends of the earth" (v. 21 and cf. Is 60).

The Jubilees text, however, makes another point. It is not only the sons of Abraham who are chosen. Even though Ishmael and Esau were direct descendants of Abraham (and circumcised, though this is not mentioned or considered here), God did not choose them "for he knew them." Simple descent from Abraham is not enough. Rather the sons of Israel are gathered from all the sons of man because there are many nations and many people. Such questions are also reflected on in groups contemporary with Jesus, not least among the Essenes at Qumran, who had copies of Jubilees in their library, and who developed what was an admittedly extreme form of Jewish response to questions of membership.

Qumran believed that only a small group of Jews, a remnant, would be saved. This notion of a remnant is linked to the Covenant in a way that has plenty of scriptural warrant. "But when he remembered the covenant with the men of former times he left a remnant to Israel and did not give them to destruction" (CD 1.4–5; cf. Is 11:20–3; Zec 8:6, 11–12). Thus the community sees its members *alone* as the true heirs of the Covenant (1QH 6.7–8; CD 6.2–11). The group had been hand-picked, eternally predestined by God, and its members would, one by one, be brought into the Covenant by his grace and call. This is celebrated in the Hymns of the community that praise God:

> I thank thee, O Lord,
> for thou hast placed my soul
> in the bundle of the living
> and hast hedged me about
> against all the Snares of the Pit.
> (1QH 2.20–1)

Quite specifically, those who were called into the community in this way had to swear an oath by which they undertook to separate themselves from all evil and to "cling to all his commandments according to his will" (1QS 5.1). Becoming a member of the community was seen as separation from the congregation of the men of falsehood and as uniting, with respect to the Law and possessions, under the authority of the sons of Zadok, the priests who keep the Covenant (1QS 5.1–3). It required a conscious voluntary decision; full membership was achieved only after a period of instruction and testing.

This marks a very important shift in the understanding of the basic Jewish concepts of election and covenant. Election is not an event in Israel's past, the benefits of which are transmitted by physical descent; it is now an eternal event that is communicated directly to individual Jews. The Covenant – of grace – is between God and those whom he has chosen from among the Jewish people. It certainly has its roots in the Law given to Moses; but it is only those to whom the true understanding of that Law has been given, "the priests who keep the Covenant" (as distinct from the Wicked Priest and his servants in the Temple), who may inherit the promises. This radical interpretation of election and covenant is marked by changes in names. The faithful are referred to as "men of the community," as "saints," "sons of righteousness" (1QS 3.20): as ruled by the Prince of Light (1QS 3.20). It is clear then that they see the boundaries of *true* Jewishness as coinciding with their own.

By redefining the group in this way Qumran could begin to make sense of the darker side of Israel's history. The history of Israel's apostasy that had brought oppression upon them was to be explained in terms of God's eternal predestination. He had set two spirits over humanity: a spirit of truth and a spirit of falsehood (1QS 3.17–19). Only the "men of the community" were ruled by the Prince of Light (1QS 3.20). Others, including prominent Jewish kings and high priests, were in fact dominated by a spirit of falsehood. They were liars and preachers of lies (1QpHab 10.9). This of course contrasts very interestingly with Jubilees' doctrine of evil spirits leading the nations astray while God alone rules over Israel. Even in the community at Qumran the spirit of falsehood is at work. Constant vigilance is therefore required to ward off his attacks. But this is all part of God's eternal purpose and – after much testing and a final war – he will bring his chosen people to "healing, great peace in a long life, and fruitfulness, together with every everlasting blessing and eternal joy" (1QS 4.7). Doubtless much of this theology is speculation after the event of Qumran's opting out of the main structures of Jewish social, political, economic, and religious life. But when one considers the hierarchical and tribal nature of Jewish society one can see why such a radical demonization of Jewish leaders was necessary. By setting themselves up as the sole legitimate "men of the Covenant" they were severing all connections with the traditional sources of authority and legitimacy in the group. That position could only be sustained by offering a radical reinterpretation of who those authorities were.

Qumran is an extreme example of redefining Jewish membership. Other groups, however, made interesting changes in emphasis while retaining – or at least remaining within – the traditional framework of Jewish society.

The early Zealots represent one interesting group here. The term "Zealots" is a convenient one for those who led the armed struggle against the Romans during the first century A.D. How far they were a cohesive group, based on a particular Jewish family, is debated. The history of dissensions within the Jewish opposition to the Romans suggests that it was far from united. Nevertheless it is likely that opposition groups at least held certain beliefs in common. Josephus refers to them as having their own "philosophy" (*Ant.* xviii.9) and attributes this to an early figure, Judas the Galilean, who featured in the disturbances after Herod's death in 4 B.C. and led the revolt against the census in A.D. 6 (*Ant.* xvii.271–7, xviii. 23–5; *War* ii.117–19).

Judas, we are told in the *Jewish War*, "incited his countrymen to revolt, upbraiding them as cowards for consenting to pay tribute to the Romans and tolerating mortal masters after having God for their Lord" (*War* ii.118). At this point Josephus stressed the difference between Judas' and other Jewish schools. In the *Antiquities*, however, we are told that the Zealots' opinions agreed in all respects with the Pharisees' "except that they have a passion for liberty that is almost unconquerable, since they are convinced that God alone is their leader and master" (*Ant.* xviii.23). It is right to see Judas and his followers as in most senses traditionalists. They believed in the Covenant and the Law and the land. God had given the land to Israel, and it was for Israel to struggle for its liberation from foreign domination. What is interesting here is the dominant metaphor that they chose to apply to the relationship between Jews and God; namely, that between subjects and their king.

In itself there is nothing very unusual about Jews speaking about God as King. More interesting and innovative is the way that God is spoken of as sole King by contrast with all other earthly kings. This is certainly new: Jews had accepted the existence and indeed rule of foreign kings often enough in the past. It is interesting too insofar as it incorporates a particular kind of oppositional element into Jews' understanding of themselves. Jews are subjects of their king Yahweh – and *not* of any other king.

Acknowledgment of and obedience to other kings is disloyalty to God. In short, the true Jew is one whose obedience to God leads him to oppose all those who falsely claim domination over Israel. Equally, Jews who comply with such false kings are faithless subjects and deserving of punishment. We shall look at the more detailed implications of this later.

If the Zealots gave interesting twists to the traditional notion of kingship, other groups appear to have placed greater emphasis on the cult and associated notions of purity. Strictly speaking this is perhaps more a matter of maintaining one's relation to God than of membership itself. A *true* Jew is one who keeps himself and his group free from alien influence and who is bound to God through worship in the Temple – above all through the great festivals of Passover, Weeks, and Tabernacles and through the daily sacrifices and the ritual of Yom Kippur (the Day of Atonement).

For the Sadducees, the aristocratic (*Ant.* xviii.16–17) priestly party that largely controlled the Temple (Acts 5:17; *Ant.* xx.199), this was doubtless the single most important feature of Jewish life. It was the point at which God's relation to Israel became a reality, as it was the central point of the system of sacrifices or offerings that had been established after the return from exile by Ezra and Nehemiah and which was enshrined in the Pentateuch. Maintenance of this system was essential for the well-being of the nation, and participation in it was essential for those who wished to fulfill the Covenant.

We know from Josephus that the Sadducees were a minority party and much opposed by the Pharisees, who had more support from the people (*Ant.* xviii.17). It is likely that such opposition only hardened their own attitudes by making them the more opposed to any modification of the tradition. Thus it is likely that for them Jewishness was indeed defined in traditional terms: membership of the Jewish nation by virtue of descent and circumcision as prescribed by the Law, together with active participation in the cult as also therein prescribed. In all this the Sadducees effectively upheld the basic ideology of the postexilic state.

But whereas more radical groups would take to the hills to overthrow foreign rulers, the Sadducees clearly believed that it was desirable and permissible to come to terms with occupying powers, rather than risk conflict, and, as eventually occurred, the loss of the Temple itself. In this adapting to the prevailing political realities, they were of course doing no more or less than many other Jews in the Diaspora were obliged to do. And it was the measure of the success of such policies that the Temple continued to enjoy the support of all but a minority, and that it received large revenues from Jews all around the Mediterranean.

But again, three hundred years of occupation and foreign domination had undermined Jewish confidence in such a national religion based on a Temple-state. And it was, as we have seen, during this period that some groups, notably the Pharisees, began to transfer the center of the cult from the Temple to the more local groupings of the synagogue and the home.

As we suggested in the preceding chapter, the Pharisees had their origins in the Jewish renewal groups that arose at the time of the Maccabean revolt. Although originally they had sought to exercise influence through the Jewish aristocracy, it is clear that by the first century they had begun to make the move from "politics to piety" (J. Neusner) to exploit their considerable popular support in local communities, through the local law courts and synagogues. Their chief concern was with the implementation of the Law, with preserving Jewish identity by embracing all aspects of life under the Law. In this way Jews could effectively distance themselves from alien ways. Moreover, certain rules, dietary laws, and avoidance rules served very effectively to separate observant Jews from their gentile neighbors.

One of the interesting features of this move was the way purity regulations, like the washing of hands (cf. Mk 7:1–8; Sifre on Nm 18:17; b.Shab. 14b), which previously had applied to the Temple priests, were now applied in the context of family meals. Of this more later, but it deserves mention here because it shows a new awareness of the focus of group identity. Jews were Jews not solely as members of a nation with its center at Jerusalem. They were members of a religious group within the Hellenistic world whose center was in the prayer and worship in the home and the local congregation. And because in the world of the cities, at least, they lived in an often predominantly alien culture, it was necessary for them to mark themselves out from the surrounding world.

Certainly for the Pharisees, membership of local groups would not have been purely a matter of birth and descent, important though these were. In the first place, Pharisees encouraged proselytes, provided they were willing to accept the Law, including circumcision (b.Shab. 31a; Mt 23:15). But even for those born Jews, descent and circumcision were not enough. Jews needed to take the yoke of the Kingdom upon themselves, actively to acknowledge and affirm God's sovereignty and rule over them. And where, if the national center was corrupt or debarred to them – or simply destroyed – should such an affirmation occur? Such questions clearly became all the more acute in the period after the fall of Jerusalem in A.D. 70. This marks the real emergence of Pharisaism as the dominant force in Jewish piety. Its initial instrument was the Academy at Jamnia, a city of mixed population near the coast. It was here that the intensive study of the Law was pursued, which led to the codification of the teaching of the sages in the Mishnah. The leading figure in the immediate aftermath of the fall was Rabbi Johanan ben Zakkai. He taught: "If one desires to take upon oneself the yoke of the kingdom of heaven in the most complete manner, one should relieve oneself, wash one's hands, and put on *tephillin* and recite the *Shema'*, and say the *tephillah*: this is the complete acknowledgement of the kingdom of heaven" (b.Ber. 14b, 15a). It is in the "sanctuary" of the home that the Jew acknowledges and affirms the rule of God.

Such transitions – from Pharisees at court to the Judaism of post-70 based on home and synagogue – are not easy to trace. The main Jewish sources were all written after the fall of Jerusalem and doubtless reflect subsequent developments, even when they refer to events of the earlier part of the century.

Thus it is not easy to know how far Pharisaic influence had spread during the time of Jesus, nor to know how far they saw themselves – like the Essenes – as being the only true Jews. On the face of it, it is most unlikely that they were so exclusive. Any Jewish group that was seeking to influence the affairs of the nation was hardly likely to have regarded those outside their own party as excluded from Israel. We do, however, hear of one group: the *haberim*, who certainly observed very strict dietary rules and rules of table fellowship and, according to the later records, distanced themselves from other less observant Jews. "A *haber* does not enter the house of an *'am ha-'arez* (literally: "a person of the land," an ignorant, nonobservant Jew) and does not accept him as a guest if the latter wears his own garments" (m. Dem 2.3). Some scholars believe that in fact the *haberim* were identical with the Pharisees and that they constituted an exclusive sect regarding themselves – and themselves only – as the true heirs of the Covenant, who represented the true community of Israel. Others regard the *haberim* as a more sectarian grouping within the Pharisaic movement. Given the acknowledged diversity of the Pharisees (there were well-known schools of Shammai and Hillel) and the other, historical considerations, the latter view is more likely. However difficult it may be to discover the exact nature of Pharisaic belief and practice during the period prior to A.D. 70, one thing can be said with some confidence. Pharisees were concerned in what was a major exercise in the reconstruction of Judaism. For them questions about membership were fundamental ones about what it really meant to be a Jew, asked at a time when there was increasing pressure on traditional ways. In order to meet such pressures, they needed to restate, to redefine in some degree what it was to be a Jew. This is clear from their emphasis on the oral tradition, which is acknowledged to be, in part at least, innovative (b.Shab. 14b), and from the great burst of creative work in the period after A.D. 70.

They were concerned to work out a new identity for Jews living in a predominantly alien culture. What they achieved was a shift from a national folk religion to a form of communal piety.

Another way of looking at group membership deserves mention and that is found in a figure like John the Baptist. Christians have of course traditionally viewed John as a forerunner of the Christ (Mk 1:2–3) and therefore as part of the Christian order of things. From another point of view he is very much part of the contemporary Jewish religious scene and is reported by Josephus as such (*Ant.* xviii.116–19). John is a national prophet of renewal. He called Jews to repent and be baptized in order to prepare for the stronger one who would come with fire and spirit (Mt 3:11). In this John has clearly drawn on prophetic traditions of calls to national repentance. But there are at least indications that he was also in a sense redefining group boundaries.

In the first place it is certain that for John repentance and baptism were more important than Jewish descent and circumcision. Only those who repented and were baptized and bore fruits worthy of repentance would be saved (Mt 3:1–8). The others were doomed, for the ax was already laid at the root of the tree (Mt 3:10). Thus those who are not with him are effectively out, which may explain the Pharisees' edginess about John. But it may be that John went even further than that. According to Matthew (3:9) and Luke (3:8), John attacked those who relied on Jewish descent – on their status as "sons of Abraham." God can raise up children to Abraham out of these stones. What is needed is repentance and the fruits of repentance. Now that may be a prophetic exaggeration: simply emphasizing the need for repentance and not seriously suggesting that Jewish descent is irrelevant. But there are other indications in Luke at least that John went further.

Luke gives more detail of John's ethical teaching and there

are two striking features about it. First, it is addressed, in part
at least, to those who have at best marginal status within Judaism: tax collectors and soldiers (Lk 3:12–13). What is more,
they are not told to abandon their positions, merely to act
moderately and justly. Second, the advice given is cast in broad
ethical terms and makes no specific reference to the Mosaic
Law. Luke may be putting his own slant on the traditional
material he has in common with Matthew. But if it should
reflect accurately the Baptist's teaching it would suggest (1)
that he was prepared to offer baptism and forgiveness of sins to
all who were ready to repent, including non-Jews; (2) that by
contrast with the rabbis, who required of proselytes that they
should accept the whole Law, John was prepared to accept those
who lived in accordance with values widely taught in the
Hellenistic world.

We have to be cautious with this kind of analysis. John was
clearly a millenarian prophet preaching principally to Jews. But
he speaks as one at the end of the ages who therefore looks
beyond the traditions of his fathers to a new age. What matters,
in the light of the imminence of the new age, is to repent and do
good, above all to be ready for what is to come. And in principle
at least, anyone who is prepared to do that can come in.

Such a reading of John is at least encouraged by a comparison
and contrast with Jubilees. Baptism in John seems to function
very similarly to circumcision in Jubilees, namely, as a seal or
sign against the coming judgment and destruction (Jub. 15.26),
perhaps after the manner of the blood on the doorposts in Egypt
(Ex 12:13). Only those who repent and are baptized are to be
numbered among the chosen, just as only the circumcised will
avoid destruction. That is to say, baptism here *replaces* circumcision as the condition of salvation and of membership of the
group – and this is clearly more acceptable to non-Jews. Moreover one might also recall how, even in Jubilees, membership of
Israel is drawn from all the "sons of man." Even within quite

fiercely exclusive groupings we should not automatically expect a strong racial or national bias.

There is, then, among the various groups and figures of first-century Judaism a very considerable diversity of understanding of what it is to be Jewish, more specifically of what it is to be a member of the people of God. While Jewish descent and circumcision are fundamental signs of membership of the people with whom the Covenant has been made, that is certainly not the sole condition. In the end these variations can be classified in terms of their acceptance, modification, or rejection of the Jewish nation-state. In the middle there are the Sadducees, who work firmly within the framework of the Temple-state: participation in the national cult is what enables a Jew to affirm and acknowledge his Jewishness. Then at one extreme there is a figure like John the Baptist, who –at least on Luke's reading – seems poised to open the borders of Judaism to all those of goodwill who are ready to repent and do good works, even to those in the service of foreign powers and client rulers. By contrast there are those who wish to narrow, to sharpen the definition of what it is *really* to be a Jew: the Zealots, who see all those who acknowledge or serve foreign rulers as faithless subjects; the Pharisees, who start regrouping the people of God around the synagogue and home; the *haberim*, who set up sharp cultic boundaries around their group; the Essenes, who consign all those outside their group, Jews and Gentiles alike, to the Prince of Darkness.

Where then does Jesus stand on this scale? The question is not often asked in this manner and is not at all easy to answer. On the one hand there are important links and similarities between Jesus and John the Baptist. He was, after all, originally John's disciple. Like John, Jesus expected the coming of a new age, the Kingdom, and therefore the ending of this present age (Mk 9:1). In that sense he stands in line with those who looked for some fairly radical transformation of Judaism, its restoration, if you like, but in a renewed form. The question then is, who would be included in the "new" Judaism? What would its structures be, and where would its center be?

As far as membership is concerned, we have two apparently contradictory indications: on the one hand, Jesus invited sinners and tax collectors into the Kingdom and ate with them (Mk 2:13–17). He commanded his followers to "love their enemies" (Mt 5:44) – those outside – and he looked to a time when "many will come from the East and West" (Mt 8:11). On the other hand he restricted his mission and that of his disciples to the "lost sheep of the house of Israel" (Mt 15:24). Did Jesus simply look forward to a national renewal when *Jews* would return to the faith of their forebears? Or did he look forward to a more radical renewal of the people of God, who would then be open to the Gentiles, who in turn would be drawn to the light (Is 60)? If the latter, then there is nothing contradictory about his *initial* restriction of his work to the people of Israel. Membership of the renewed people of God – when once it was renewed – would be open to all.

But what were the structures of the "new" Israel to be? Was it to be based on the old dynastic and tribal patterns and on the Temple? The answers to that will have to wait till a later chapter. Here we may point to the fact that Jesus' choice of twelve disciples to sit on the twelve thrones of Israel and his onslaught on the Temple indicate a fairly radical revision of patterns of authority and distribution of power. Power is to be taken from the old families and given to a band of Galilean peasants. The Temple is to be destroyed. A new kingdom with its roots in the powerless, the faithless, and the collaborators is to replace the old order. It is small wonder that such a message stirred deep opposition from both Jewish and Roman leaders.

In this Jesus was clearly looking forward to a quite radical renewal of Judaism, and in this he was like the Pharisees. But unlike them he appears to have been less concerned with a detailed reconstruction of the forms of Jewish piety and more concerned to point to radical new values that he advocated as the values of the coming Kingdom.

Chapter 4

Setting Priorities and Maintaining Group Standards

Defining who belonged to the group was one way of coping with some of the pressures on first-century Judaism. The group's resilience could always be reinforced by defining out some of the weaker or more faithless members or by offering a renewed vision of what it was to be a Jew. Setting priorities for members' behavior and devising ways of reinforcing such behavior, were other, related ways of enabling the group to withstand the erosion of its values and norms.

There is, of course, a measure of overlap here with the previous chapter. Defining what it was to be a true Jew obviously entailed specifying what were the correct forms of behavior. What we shall be principally concerned with in this chapter are the distinctive emphases different groups made in so specifying patterns of behavior, and the strategies they devised for upholding them.

The problem here was simply this. God, so Jews believed, had chosen the people of Israel and made a contract with them: if they were faithful to his will as expressed in the Law he would be faithful to them. But in the first place the Law was complex and at times contradictory. In the second, many of its rulings had their roots in a pastoral, nomadic existence; this meant that often considerable ingenuity was required before they could be applied in first-century agrarian and urban Palestine. Furthermore alongside these difficulties inherent in the Law, there were strong forces outside straining Jews' loyalties. In Hellenism, we have seen, they were confronted by an alternative life-style that offered considerable rewards to those able to embrace it and a sense of exclusion and inadequacy to those who were not. In short, there were both internal difficulties within the Law and external forces that made observance of the Law difficult. But faithful observance was just what the more thoughtful elements considered necessary. It was because of Israel's faithlessness that they had suffered as they had. Only "zeal" for the Law (1 Mc 2:27) could restore Israel's fortunes.

There is a certain element of Catch-22 in this kind of situation. It was not easy to be a "good" Jew because the rules were complex and there were powerful counter-attractions. Equally it was not felt to be enough just to be a reasonably good Jew because one of the reasons given for the Jews' difficulties was that they had not been good enough. This then encouraged a raising of standards precisely at a time of increased difficulty in maintaining existing ones.

Yet if that kind of response seems in some ways to be trying to make difficulties for oneself, it is understandable enough. Any threat to a group's standards is likely to lead to a reassertion and reexamination of group values.

Interestingly of course such "zeal for the Law" – such a determination to enforce group values – can have very different outcomes. Some will want to redouble their efforts to observe all the regulations; others will prefer to stress certain aspects of the Law that it is essential to observe at all costs. That is to say, one way of responding to difficulties in sustaining group norms is to develop strategies that stiffen the group's resolve; another way is to reassess one's priorities and to concentrate attention on specific aspects of the tradition. Such moves are not, of course, mutually exclusive.

The Sadducees and the True Temple Worship

It is easy to misrepresent the Sadducees. They may appear simply as a reactionary group, concerned only to maintain their position as hereditary rulers and resistant to all change. In a sense that is true. They held important offices in the Temple and were principally concerned to ensure the continuance of the Temple cult. They rejected the Pharisees' belief that God had given Moses not only the written Law but also an oral Law that contained the key to its interpretation. They rather concentrated their attention on the specific prescriptions of the Pentateuch: "They own no observation of any sort apart from the Laws" (*Ant.* xviii.16). Instead, they tried to keep to the strict letter of the Law. To be more precise, they were concerned with the strict letter of the Law relating to the central institutions and structures of the Temple-state: the Temple cult and the priesthood. In this they had to operate with an institution, the Sanhedrin, or Council, which ruled on matters of Law and which, ironically, was not even mentioned in the Law. However that may be, their loyalties lay with the Temple.

In all this the Sadducees remained essentially faithful to the order of things that had been established by Ezra on the return from exile in Babylon in the fifth century B.C. and which was enshrined in the Pentateuch. It was a form of Judaism that was theoretically theocratic, established by divine decree given to Moses, and administered by the priests. Practically it had been established by grace of the Persian kings Cyrus and Darius (Ezr 1:1–4 and 6:1–12) and would always be more or less dependent on the favor of its foreign overlords.

Thus the price of trying to hold on to the ideal of a Jewish temple-state involved compromise with the political realities of the times. In the first century A.D., the Sadducees had to accept that the high priest was appointed by the Roman governors and that the Temple was overseen by Roman soldiers. National independence had to take second place to the preservation of those national institutions that maintained Israel's relation to God. For it was the Temple cult that enabled Israel to atone for its sins and to renew its covenanted relation with

God. So long as the Temple existed, the link between God and his people could be maintained, despite all foreign interference, which doubtless explains why the Sadducees disappeared once the Temple was destroyed.

It may be tempting to suppose that just because the Sadducees were prepared to accept a measure of compromise they were less rigorous than other groups. And that may well have been how other groups saw them. But it is not necessarily the way they saw themselves. Their efforts went into rigorously maintaining the old ways of the Temple priesthood. Everything else was secondary. Numerous stories are recorded of their disputes with the Pharisees over such details of Temple ritual. Thus there was fierce debate about whether the incense to be burned on the Day of Atonement should be kindled outside or inside the Holy of Holies (b.Yom. 19b; T. Yom. 1.8). The Sadducees maintained that it should be outside. Leviticus 16:1–2 spoke of the cloud appearing "above the cover," and the Sadducees argued that this could occur only if the incense gave off its smoke outside, that is, if it was kindled outside. It was, moreover, a hazardous undertaking to light the incense inside the dark chamber, dressed in inflammable garments! So they had an interest in upholding what they saw as the literal meaning of the Law. The Pharisees, however, appealed to Leviticus 16:12f. to argue that the incense should be sprinkled on the coals in the censer inside the Holy of Holies. Such a story illustrates the Sadducees' concern not merely for self-preservation but also for strict maintenance of liturgical traditions. In this concentration on the administration of the cult they were typical of a number of groups. Rather than insisting on redoubling their efforts to fulfill all the Law, they concentrated on certain aspects of the Law, in this case the part that governed the Temple cult. They sought a way out of Israel's problems by underlining those aspects of the Law that they considered essential.

The Zealots and Their Search for National Independence

If the Sadducees were prepared to accept loss of national sovereignty so long as they kept control of the Temple, the Zealots were not. Their heroes were the Maccabees, who had purified the Temple only after overcoming the oppressor, an action, moreover, that went hand in hand with fortifying it "with high walls and strong towers round about, to keep the Gentiles from trampling them down as they had before" (1 Mc 4:36–61). This would contrast sharply with the state of affairs in the early first century when Romans occupied the towers overlooking the Temple. The true Jew for the Zealots was one who acknowledged as his king God, and God alone (*Ant.* xviii.23). Service of foreign kings was itself an act of faithlessness to the one and only king.

Thus for the Zealots, service of God meant striving for freedom from foreign domination. They had, Josephus tells us, "a passion for liberty that is almost unconquerable" (*Ant.* xviii.23). What we know of them is quite specific but doubtless not comprehensive. We have only short accounts from Josephus that are not even entirely self-consistent. They objected particularly to the census imposed on Jews after the deposition of Archelaus in A.D. 6 (*Ant.* xviii.3–10; *War* ii.118). This census was to form the basis of a property tax and both submitting to the census and paying taxes were seen as acts of acknowledging the rule of Rome and submitting to slavery (*Ant.* xviii.4). The conflict over paying taxes to Caesar was clearly still a live one at the time of Jesus' ministry some twenty years later (Mk 12:13–17). Memories of the revolt at the time of the census would have led Jews to ask, if our fathers died rather than submit to the census, should we now pay taxes?

Alongside the specific commands neither to pay taxes nor to submit to the census there were certain injunctions of a more general character. The Jews were called to strive for freedom. This might well mean answering the call of an inspired leader to leave all that one had and to go up into the hills to fight (*War* ii.118). It might mean being prepared to give one's life for the cause and to face torture and martyrdom. The terrible tortures inflicted on Jews during the revolt against Antiochus Epiphanes in the second century B.C. were clearly fascinating (see especially 2 Mc 6 and 7) and would have served as inspiration to those fighting for freedom in the first century.

The call for freedom from foreign domination, linked with notions of zeal for the Law, would have certainly also entailed keeping oneself apart from all alien influences. Here it is more than likely that the figure of Phinehas, celebrated in the Maccabean literature, and indeed in late rabbinic writing, will have acted as a popular inspiration. Loyal Jews should be zealous as Phinehas, who had speared Zimri and the Midianite woman the latter had introduced into the camp (Nm 25). Such notions may have inspired the later campaign of political assassination that Josephus sets in the mid-fifties (*War* ii.254–7). Members of this group earned the name of *sicarii*, derived from the Latin word for a dagger, and mingled with crowds at festivals with their weapons concealed in their clothes. Their first victim was the high priest Jonathan, seen, one may assume, as a traitor to the people because of his collaboration with the Romans.

Thus, for the Zealots the question of how to be obedient to the Law was sharply focused on questions of national independence. Their program was a long way from being a demand to fulfill all the ordinances of the Law. It was much more concerned with the achievement of certain military and political goals that would be the necessary preliminary to the restoration of the nation's independence. For them the full realization of God's Rule lay in the future, and the purification of the Temple would have to wait for the final victory. Thus we can see in the ideas of Judas the Galilean a concentration on certain essential marks of obedience that true Israelites had to show to their sole king, God. They had to refuse obedience to foreign and false kings; they had to strive for freedom and independence by all effective means including force of arms; and they must keep themselves free from all alien influence. Those who collaborated, by contrast, were to be rejected and even struck down. This constitutes a radicalization of the Jewish Law, focusing on quite specific areas that are seen as essential for the restoration of national sovereignty. Like the Sadducees, who emphasized maintenance of the cult as the essential component of obedience to God, the Zealots too emphasized certain specific elements of the Law. But unlike the Sadducees, they could not accept that God's Rule was fully acknowledged and obeyed in a Jewish state whose leaders also recognized the authority of Rome. They cherished, that is to say, a more radical ideal of a theocratic state, one moreover that had rarely if ever been realized in Israel's history since the restoration after the Exile.

John the Baptist and the Coming Reign of God

Like the Zealots, John saw the full realization of God's Rule as something for the future and therefore concentrated on certain necessary preliminaries in the present. John's teaching focused on his belief that the present age was about to come to a dramatic end with the arrival of "the stronger one." He would come to judge all people; the wicked would be destroyed and the righteous purified. All were called to repent and be baptized in order to survive the coming judgment. Those who repented should then "bear fruits worthy of repentance" (Mt 3:11–12).

John's main emphasis was clearly not so much on maintaining existing group standards as on offering a new way of life to those who felt themselves to have failed. The popularity of John's preaching, repeatedly stressed in the stories told about him, shows how deep a chord he struck. "Then went out to him Jerusalem and all Judaea and all the region about the Jordan" (Mt 3:5). Obviously many people longed for a life where they would not feel constantly frustrated, where they would be able to live in accordance with the Law and feel assured of God's goodwill.

Such feelings of frustration will have had complex roots. It is implausible to suggest that rural Palestine was simply in a state of moral decline at the time. Certainly it is most unlikely to have been the case that so many Jews were in actual flagrant breach of the Law. Why then the call to repentance? And why the deep popular response? Such popular prophetic movements indicate a loss of moral and religious confidence. A number of factors may have contributed to this. First, economic pressures made life generally difficult for peasant farmers and therefore decreased the amount of time and energy available for detailed religious observation. Second, those in rural areas may well have felt alienated from the main center of religious power in Jerusalem and from its leaders with their links to the occupying Roman power. Economically, too, the rural population was poorer and largely dependent on landlords, who belonged to the world of the large cities of Hellenistic culture. Religiously and culturally then they must have felt the gulf between themselves and the Temple aristocracy. Third, they felt the attraction of the alien culture that effectively dominated the land, and which offered a more international, a more prosperous and in many ways more open way of life. The mixture of cultures and faiths found in the cosmopolitan cities on the coast will have horrified some and attracted others.

In the face of Jews' loss of confidence in traditional mores, it would be interesting to know what kinds of standards John set for those who responded to his call. Did he insist on a strict observation of the Law? Did he anticipate a time when the old order of things would be restored, with a renewed Temple and a leadership truly of the people? None of this is reflected in our documents.

Unfortunately, there is in fact little positive indication of any kind of what John did teach. Only the Lucan material gives a possible clue. The ethical demands John makes of those who repent are cast in terms that seem as close to Greek popular philosophy as to the Law. Those who have more than they need should share with those who have too little. Tax collectors should not make extortionate profits, and soldiers should curb the use of force (Lk 3:10–14). Such things could probably have been heard from the mouths of wandering philosophers in Greek cities around the Mediterranean. Certainly John here makes no reference to matters specifically relating to the Jewish cult or to Jewish dietary regulations. Equally, those who repented were not required to abandon ways of life such as tax collecting, which would in themselves have been offensive to many Jews. They were required to share their goods justly and to act fairly and moderately in their public lives.

Perhaps what John envisaged was a future age where there would be some kind of fusion, some synthesis between Jewish and Hellenistic virtues. For many Jews, alien cultures were something to be hated and rooted out; for others their attractions were so great that they were prepared to abandon much of their own traditional way of life to reap the benefits. John looked forward to a new age when these divisions would be overcome. It would be a marriage of what is best in all cultures, a marriage blessed by God. For God, through his agent, the "stronger one," would bring in the new age.

Such a reading of John's teaching is admittedly speculative. The speculation, however, is encouraged by some general thoughts about religious and cultural change. Where there is confrontation between alien cultures different reactions are possible. In some there is simply opposition, which may be either aggressive or defensive. In others one culture becomes dominant and simply absorbs the other. But there are also occasions where there is a creative synthesis between the two, such that new religious forms and beliefs emerge. Prophetic figures like John may initiate or facilitate such creative changes by announcing the end of the present age and the coming of a new age with new rules. The new rules may reflect values drawn both from their own and from the alien culture. In that sense John is truly the forerunner of a new age. And in this, interestingly, he may be less concerned with identifying those aspects of the Law that are vital for Jewish survival than with laying down the ground rules for the new age.

The Essenes and the Fulfillment of All the Works of the Law

The Essenes provide an interesting contrast with John that may help to underline some of the points we have just made. As we have seen, this group called people out of the existing order of things into a community that saw itself as wholly distinct from everyone else, Jew and Gentile alike. They were the true sons of the Covenant whom God alone had called. This consciousness of their distinctiveness over against other Jews was linked to a sense that they were the true Jews who had the true understanding of the Law. Those who took the oath and entered the community at Qumran were required to undergo a lifetime of study of the Law. Not only was the Law studied deeply; the community enforced its observance by a strict code of discipline. Status within the community was related to proficiency in knowledge of and obedience to the Law. A man's progress was assessed annually. In all this the emphasis, constantly repeated in their writings, was on performing "all the commandments of the Law."

That is to say: Like John, the community at Qumran expected the coming of a new age. Like him too, they already saw themselves as called out from the mass of the damned in readiness for that new age. But unlike John, they conceived of that new age in terms that bore close resemblance to the old age, restored and reformed. In this respect, then, their whole life together was devised with the purpose of upholding and enforcing the Laws of the Jewish Scriptures as they understood them. Nevertheless they also interpreted the Law, or rather, administered the final interpretation of the Law that had been revealed to their founder, who is referred to in their writings as the Teacher of Righteousness.

Of course we know a lot more about the beliefs and practices of the community at Qumran than we do about John. The community also had a much longer history. In both respects the comparison with John becomes rather distorted. John may have said more about the observance of the Law than we know. Equally John did not have much time to reflect on the rules for his followers after baptism. Qumran had nearly two hundred years. Nevertheless the general point is worth emphasizing: Whereas John looked forward to an age where the community's standards and laws would be radically renewed, the community at Qumran looked forward to an age where the worship of the Temple would be restored to its former purity and where the sons of the Covenant would again inherit the land and live in accordance with all the commandments of the Law.

Meanwhile how did they live? How did they maintain their beliefs and standards? We know from excavations at the site of the community's buildings some basic facts about its life. It was a small community supporting itself by farming, living in isolation from other communities. The site is remarkable for the number of water cisterns it contains. These were necessary for the community's physical needs but also played an important part in their ritual, with its many washings. According to Josephus (*War* ii.129) the water was used for regular purification before breakfast. Only the initiated washed and entered a special room: "pure now themselves they repair to the refectory, as to some sacred shrine." This is also reflected in the sect's own writings (1QS 5.13) where it is also suggested (1QS 3.8f.) that a ritual washing formed part of the rite for initiation into full membership of the community. There was a scriptorium for copying scrolls and a refectory for common meals. All this confirms what we know from the documents: that it was a tightly knit, isolated community, whose life was focused on the study of its sacred texts.

Two aspects of the community's belief and practice should be spelled out a little more. What is it to say that it was tightly knit and that its life was centered on the study of sacred texts? The Dead Sea community kept to itself. Entry to the community was carefully controlled, and dealings with those outside were strictly regulated. Those who wished to enter the community were first examined and then had to undergo a period of probation (1QS 6.13–23). For the first two years prospective members were not allowed to enter the water or to partake of "the pure meal of the congregation." At the end of the first year and a further examination they were allowed to transfer their property to the community, where, however, it was kept in a separate account. After a further year they were again examined, given a rank within the community, and admitted to its meals. At this stage their property was merged with that of the community. All this indicates the wariness in the community about taking in people from outside.

The same wariness is to be found in their dealings with others who were not of their community. Here it is more difficult to know precisely what happened. One interesting text reads: "No member of the community shall follow them in matters of doctrine and justice, or eat and drink anything of theirs, or take anything from them except for a price" (1QS 5.16f.). This is a clear prohibition on accepting gifts of food or drink or property from those outside the community – or as it

said: "all the men of falsehood who walk in the way of wicked-
ness" (1QS 5.10–11). This would clearly prohibit the sharing of
meals with outsiders and probably also any business part-
nership. Straight purchase of goods was permitted, as this was
thought of as therefore ceasing to be the property of the former
owner *before* it was brought into the community. Clearly all
this had a wider significance. Exchange of goods and food was
prohibited as part of a policy of impeding the exchange of ideas:
"No member of the community shall follow them in matters
of doctrine and justice" (1QS 5.16). Prohibition of sharing
meals and property clearly inhibited opportunities for intellectual exchange. It also served as a powerful reminder of the need
to have nothing to do with dangerous outsiders.

Just as the community set up tight boundaries against an
alien and wicked world, so too it maintained well-defined internal boundaries. There was a clearly structured hierarchy
within the community, leading up to the council, which had
ultimate responsibility for the regulation of its affairs. Members were graded according to their understanding of and obedience to the Law, and this ranking was reviewed annually
(1QS 5.23–5). In other words, rank within the community was
a reflection of the Law's centrality to its life. The hierarchy
that was thus established was carefully safeguarded. At the
assemblies, members sat according to their status. Those of
higher rank spoke before those of lower (1QS 6.8–13). According to Josephus, accidental physical contact between persons of
different rank led to pollution such that the senior member had
to take a bath, "as after contact with an alien" (*War* ii.150).

In other ways too the community marked out its sepa-
rateness from the world and inculcated the need for watch-
fulness. There is a repeated emphasis in its writings on the
purity of the community, particularly on its meals. There was
provision for regular washings, and complicated prescriptions
for relieving oneself (*War* ii.147–9). There was, in short, a pre-

occupation with dirt and cleanliness. It is unlikely that this is merely evidence of the community's concern with hygiene; it is more likely that it was a way of marking the need to be on one's guard against the alien, against what should not be there. A community that feels itself to be an embattled minority often develops such mechanisms.

This tightly controlled structure was designed both to ensure strict adherence to the group's laws and to protect the group from outside influence. And this was necessary, partly because it was a small, isolated, and therefore vulnerable community, and partly because its whole raison d'être lay in its own special understanding of the Law, which had to be carefully preserved.

The community believed that the true meaning of the Law had been revealed to its founder, the Teacher of Righteousness (CD 1.11–12; CD 3.12–17; 1QS 1.9). All other interpretations of the Law were false and could lead the community into error. This explains the provisions about separation from all false doctrine and from all those who might pervade them. But even within the community understanding of such matters was not to be taken for granted. Hence the need for constant study and for the careful testing of members before they were allowed in to the higher echelons of the community. Hence too the very strict penalties for breaching the Law (1QS 6.24–7.25).

The literature and archaeology of the Essene community thus present us with a very clear picture of how one group in first-century Judaism tried to regulate its affairs. It made no attempt to reduce the scope of its obedience to the Law. On the contrary, it strove for perfection in its members' observance and understanding of it. It claimed, however, to have its own distinctive understanding of the Law that not only set it apart from all other Jews but disqualified the others as well. It lived almost entirely outside Jewish society, though it had visitors and was described in guides to the area (such as Pliny's *Natural History* v. 15/73). However, it had not abandoned the traditional hope for the land. That, as we shall see, would only be realized in the future.

In short, the group's strategy for maintaining its standards was threefold: a redefinition of the Law; a redoubling of efforts to observe it; and a policy of almost total separation from the rest of the – in their view – hopelessly corrupted nation.

The Pharisees and the Transfer of the Temple Cult to the Local Community

We have spent some time on the Essenes, not because they were more important than any other Jewish group, but because we know more about them, and this knowledge helps us get some kind of firm bearing on first-century Jewish society. The Pharisees showed a comparable interest in purity laws and in detailed observance of all the Law, but they were clearly more integrated into Jewish society than the Essenes. In what ways did they hope to encourage Jews to be faithful to the traditions of their forebears?

Perhaps it is helpful here to make a broad distinction. In a situation where there is erosion of a group's values, one can, broadly, choose one of two ways to combat such erosion. One is to highlight key areas of behavior and try to get these right. The other is to redouble one's efforts to fulfill all the requirements of one's group's laws. Thus religious groups in the Western Isles of Scotland who have long felt that their way of life was threatened have become stricter and more rigorous in their religious observance. This is a way of preserving one's standards: raising them to make sure that everyone takes them seriously and that, at the least, one will maintain the position from which one started.

If the Zealots tended to highlight certain areas, chiefly of political involvement, the Pharisees stressed the need to intensify one's efforts to uphold the Law. This comes out clearly in their idea of setting a hedge or fence about the Law (m.Aboth 1.1; 3.13; b.Ber. 22a). The written laws of the Pentateuch were supplemented with a more detailed set of requirements contained in the oral tradition of the Law, which protected the principle itself. Thus there are discussions about the quantity of water required to purify a man who has had a recent emission. The amount of water required, it is argued, varies depending on whether he is immersed in it or whether it is poured over him. This practice of washing is said to provide a fence against sexual misdemeanors (b.Ber. 22a). And, more generally, study of the Torah became central to the life of the community. The Pharisees developed their own tradition of interpretation (thought to have been handed down directly from Moses) that was developed through teaching and debate. All this served to focus attention on the need for careful attention to matters of the Law.

By contrast with Qumran, however, there seems to have been greater freedom of debate among the Pharisees. Not all teachers in this tradition were agreed on every point of interpretation. There is a famous story of a proselyte who went to the leaders of the two main Pharisaic schools in Herod's reign and asked them to tell him the essence of the Law while he stood on one leg. Shammai, the leader of the more rigorous school, chased him out of his workshop for his impudence. Hillel, the more accommodating leader of the other school, told him to do nothing to others that he would not want them to do to him *and that the rest of the Law lay in the interpretation of that command.* Both insisted that one must practice the whole Law, but their willingness to lead people into its proper performance was very different (b.Shab. 31a).

And there were other disputes, not least the celebrated debate between Shammai and Hillel on the grounds for divorce. Here the debate turned on the meaning of the phrase "indecency in anything" (Revised Standard Version: "some indecency":

Dt 24:1), which was said to be grounds for a man divorcing his wife. Shammai (m.Gitt. 9.10) took it to mean chastity, emphasizing the strict meaning of "indecency"; Hillel took it as permission for divorce "even if she spoiled a dish for him," stressing the sense "indecency in *anything*." The latter view seems much closer to the popular practice that is probably reflected in Josephus (*Ant.* iv.253): "for whatsoever cause – and many such may arise." The Mishnah records disputes between Shammai and Hillel in some cases only to overrule them by later sayings. For "none should persist in their opinion, for the 'fathers of the world' did not persist in their opinion" (m.Eduy 1.4). Such an approach has enabled Judaism to survive over the ages.

Inevitably such concentration on maintaining group standards leads to a greater self-consciousness on the part of the group itself. People who want to maintain their own standards do not want to have them adulterated by those of other groups. One of the ways of doing this is to build up one's group's own distinctive institutions. The emergence of the Pharisees in the first century as the dominant Jewish party saw the development of the synagogue as the center of Jewish worship and education. It was in such local meetings (whether held in special buildings or not) and in the family that the understanding of the Law was to be taught. Once the Temple was destroyed this process of regrouping around the local communities would proceed apace.

Along with attempts to strengthen the local communities went a development of purity regulations like but unlike those at Qumran. What appears to have happened (and here, as elsewhere, we are dependent on much later sources) was that regulations that applied specifically to the Temple priesthood were now applied to the home and to the fellowship. Thus washing of hands before meals (which originally applied to the Temple priesthood) was now required of all devout Jews (m.Hag. 2.5; b.Ber. 14b, 15a; b.Shab. 14b; Sifre on Nm 18:7). Prayer was to be preceded by a process of ritual purification and robing. What was happening was that the home or the local group was being compared to, and in a sense equated with, the sanctuary of the Temple. In the same way that the Temple had to be fenced off and protected from what was alien (at least in its inner sanctuary), so too must the home.

This is not by any means the same kind of exclusivism that characterized Qumran. After all, even the Temple had the Court of the Gentiles. What these practices did, however, was set a firm boundary around the local Jewish community to enable it to preserve its identity. There had to be some point in their lives that was truly the meeting place between the people and their God. It is this that had to be preserved from outside influence, for it was from this point that the community would draw the strength to fulfill God's will.

Amidst such diversity of Jewish belief and practice where are we to place Jesus? Was he closer to those sects, like Qumran and the Pharisees, who sought to counter the erosion of group norms by redoubling their efforts to uphold and to teach the whole Law, marking the group off from others around them? Was he more like the Sadducees and the Zealots, who concentrated attention on certain sections of the Law that they saw to be essential to the maintenance or restoration of Jewish life? Or was he more like John the Baptist, a prophetic figure announcing a new age with a new ethic?

It is not possible to give a simple answer to these questions. Like John and like the Zealots, Jesus focuses attention on certain key points of ethical behavior: love of God, love of neighbor, love of enemies. But on other points he can be compared to the rabbis. His summary of the Law (Mt 7:12) is similar to Hillel's reply to the proselyte; his ruling on divorce (Mt 5:32; Mk 10:2–12, etc.) bears an interesting resemblance to the debate between Hillel and Shammai. But there are also differences. Jesus does not emphasize, as do both Hillel and Shammai, the importance of performing all the works of the Law; rather he asserts that his summary is the Law and the prophets (Mt 7:12). Similarly in Mark 10:2–9 he plays off one text of Scripture against another, whereas in Mark 7:15, "there is nothing outside a man which by going into him can defile him," he rejects the purity regulations that played an important part in the life both of Qumran and the Pharisees.

It is therefore mistaken to see Jesus simply as a rather freer kind of Hillel. Such a view would do justice neither to Hillel nor to Jesus. In a sense Jesus is more like John the Baptist, a prophetic figure who looks forward to a new age and calls people to break their ties with the present age. What he announces are rules for the new Kingdom – but ones that have to be lived out in the present because that Kingdom is already dawning. In this sense he is like but unlike the Zealots. He, like them, recognizes the authority of God's Rule and the need for the faithful to obey him radically now. Like them he realizes that God's sovereignty is in an important sense impugned and looks to its full realization in the near future. Unlike them he does not believe that it can be brought about by the military defeat of the Romans, indeed by military means at all. On the contrary, because it is a peaceable kingdom, because God is a God of peace, his subjects must love, not destroy, their enemies. If they follow him along that difficult road they will both lose their life and find it in the coming of the Kingdom with power.

Chapter 5

Hopes for the Future

The picture of Judaism that has emerged over the preceding two chapters is that of a religion with a considerable internal dynamism. Although surrounded by a powerful alien culture, it nevertheless reacted to this culture variously and vigorously. The many groups that we have looked at all sought a way forward through their present difficulties. What then did they look forward to?

Precise answers to this question cannot easily be given. In the first place such hopes are often far from sharply focused intimations of a future state that serve more to stir the will than to inform. A group may well be vigorously determined not to be defeated by the forces that threaten to overwhelm it; but this does not mean that it will therefore know precisely what is to come when the struggle is over.

And further, it is not easy to map specific and distinct sets of beliefs about the future on to each of the religious groups we have been considering. Certainly there are in the contemporary literature vivid depictions of future states that had their origin in a particular group. But such visions still owed a great deal to the general stock of images of the future current at the time and themselves then contributed to that general store on which members of all groups drew from time to time.

Nor would a particular group's hopes necessarily have remained unchanged over a prolonged period. The more dramatic visions of cosmic conflict and upheaval perhaps gripped the imagination more tightly in times of crisis and oppression. But equally they may have provided strange comfort to those who, even in times of relative quiet, felt powerless and marginalized, ousted from the center of their nation's life. To such people visions of divine intervention may have served to reassure them of their worth, at least in the eyes of the Lord of Hosts.

Thus while we shall consider the particular hopes and aspirations of the various Jewish parties of the time, we shall also have to look at the visions found in the writings that have no clear association with any particular group. Above all, we should not assume that there is necessarily a very tight fit between a group's values and self-understanding and its hopes for the future. Rather we should ask what the nature of that relationship is.

The Sadducees

One group, the Sadducees, stands out. They are known to us more by what they did not hope for than what they did. The Sadducees, unlike the Pharisees and Jesus, did not believe in resurrection. "As for the persistence of the soul after death, penalties in the underworld, and rewards," Josephus tells us, "they will have none of them" (*War* ii.165; *Ant.* xviii.16; Mk 12:18–27). That is to say, they rejected belief in some *general* transformation of all things when the dead would rise and all would meet their maker and be judged.

The Sadducees have been served badly by history. They did not survive, and so we know about them only from opponents who did. Why did they reject such exciting hopes? Were they simply impious, doubting God's power over the living and the dead? This seems implausible, but to answer the question we need to reconsider the circumstances in which such beliefs in resurrection first arose.

The first clear instance of such belief comes, as we saw in Chapter 2, in Daniel 12. Faced with the suffering and martyrdom of many faithful Jews, yet buoyed by hopes of a great coming kingdom, Daniel dreams of the day when the dead will rise again to reap the reward of their deeds. If God's right-eousness is to be upheld, then there has to be recompense for those who have died before the time. But belief in rewards and punishment in a future state beyond this life really represents a radically new understanding of God's election of Israel and his Covenant and promises. For the promises are no longer to be fulfilled in the normal order of life in the land of Israel, but in some future state when, after a cosmic battle, Israel's enemies will be defeated and the dead will rise, "some to everlasting life, and some to everlasting shame and contempt" (Dn 12:2). Quite how this future state of affairs was envisaged, it is hard to say. Probably it bore considerable resemblance to the pro-phetic visions of a renewed Israel (cf., e.g., Is 60; Ez 40–7). But even if the new Israel was in one sense continuous with the past, in another it would only come after a radical transforma-tion of the present order; and it was this that the Sadducees rejected.

There is at least one good reason why the Sadducees would have been less than happy with such beliefs. Even though the Romans occupied the land, Jews still lived there and held the crucial offices in the Temple and Sanhedrin. The Sadducees still believed that the present order of things was what God had promised to Israel and that so long as the cult was maintained the means of redemption were at hand. To have suggested that only in a radically transformed order of things would God's Rule be realized would have impugned the present order in which they had too full a stake. Thus they rejected such radical hopes for the future.

Much more than this we cannot say. Doubtless the Sad-ducees looked forward to the day when they would have full control over the affairs of the Temple, when they would no longer be subject to interference from external powers. But his-tory tells us very little of all that. We know them only as the party that attempted to make the present system work as well as it could within the political constraints of the times. When the linchpin of the system, the Temple, was destroyed in A.D. 70, their world collapsed and they disappeared from history. Hoping that problems will simply go away may be no more, indeed may be less, realistic than dreaming of a new world.

The Pharisees

If the Sadducees rejected belief in the resurrection, the Pharisees affirmed it (*War* ii.163; *Ant.* xviii.14). But the question then is, what precisely did they affirm?

Two difficulties confront us: (1) knowing what was actually believed by the Pharisees at the time of Jesus, as opposed to what was attributed to them afterward; (2) knowing how to interpret the various statements attributed to them.

We can start by looking at the text of one of the central prayers of the post-70 period, the Eighteen Benedictions. This is the prayer Rabbi Johanan ben Zakkai, the leader of the Jews after the fall of Jerusalem, commanded Jews to recite if they wished to take the yoke of the Kingdom upon themselves (b.Ber. 14b, 15a). Known as the Shemoneh 'Esreh, it occurs in two main versions, one Palestinian, one Babylonian, which have an identifiable common core dating back to the time of the fall of Jerusalem. The versions differ but each expresses certain clear hopes for the future.

Both versions pray for the gathering together of the dispersed:

Proclaim our liberation with the great trumpet, and raise a banner to gather together our dispersed. . . . Blessed art thou, Lord, who gatherest the banished of thy people Israel.

Each version also prays for the restoration of Jerusalem, the renewal of the Temple, and the reestablishment of the throne of David. They differ on some points here, notably over the question of the Messiah. The Babylonian version prays specifically: "Cause the shoot of David to shoot forth quickly, and raise up his horn by thy salvation"; the Palestinian version prays that God be merciful to "the kingship of the house of David, thy righteous Messiah."

At a very simple level one might say that both versions share a belief in the restoration of the people of Israel to the land, to enjoy it fully. This means gathering in the dispersed; it means the reconstitution of Jerusalem and of the monarchy. How all that is to happen is much less clear. What its relation is to some kind of military struggle, to the coming of a powerful messiah/leader is also left open. So too is the question of Israel's future relation to the nations. But the hope for future deliverance and full enjoyment of the Jewish heritage is clearly expressed.

Some of the questions left open may have been answered in terms similar to those of the various writings of the period (from the time of Daniel, 175 B.C., to the end of the first century B.C.) that describe the end; the Sibylline Oracles (an Alexandrian text of the second century B.C.), 1 Enoch (in part second century B.C.), the Dead Sea Scrolls, the Psalms of Solomon. Even a cursory glance at such writings gives one a clear idea of the diversity. Just as Daniel spoke of some great battle whereby the nation's enemies would be overthrown, so too did the section in the Sibylline Oracles (3.652–795). Here a messianic figure, often identified with one of the Egyptian Ptolemies, is described as a divine savior (3.652–68). But in the next section the battle is described in terms that are no longer purely historical. God will speak and judgment will come on the nations. Fiery swords will fall from heaven on the earth. Destruction on a cosmic scale will come on all the wicked. "All the impious will bathe in blood" (3.669–701).

Similarly the Book of Enoch has visions of a war with the

Gentiles (1 En. 90.1–19): "A great sword was given to the sheep; and the sheep proceeded against all the beasts of the field in order to kill them." Then a throne is erected and God judges, casting the wicked into the abyss (1 En. 90:20–7). Jerusalem is transformed, the buildings refashioned, and the Jews restored to honor, with the Gentiles paying them homage (vv. 28–36). Again there is here a mixture of historical reference and cosmic nightmare. The whole is couched in allegorical terms, with Israel and the nations being represented by different animals.

By contrast the Psalms of Solomon, a work that probably dates from the time of Pompey (63–48 B.C.), is more restrained, more peaceable, but also nourishes grand hopes for the future. Psalm 17 prays for and foretells a king who will gather a holy people (v. 26) and have Gentile nations serving under his yoke (v. 30). He will not rely on horse and rider and bow (v. 33), but will be compassionate to all the nations (v. 34).

In all these various accounts of what will come there is a great variety of views about the extent to which what comes will be a continuation, though in a superior mode, of the present historical order or how far it will be a reality of a totally different kind. Talk of resurrection clearly indicates a substantially different reality. But even so, what is hoped for is often spoken of in surprisingly this-worldly terms.

The important point to note is that Jews of the Pharisaic persuasion could have filled out the terms of the Eighteen Benedictions in a variety of ways without fear of being accused of heresy. Within that permitted variety there were views about when the end would come, under what conditions, about the fate of the Gentiles, and about the discontinuity between this age and the next.

Of course there is nothing very surprising in all this. The history of a community's beliefs about the future can show remarkable change over time. Certainly this is true of Christianity, which started with an expectation of an imminent end to all things and has subsequently allowed nearly two thousand years to elapse without surrendering its central beliefs.

This is not to say that it makes no difference at all what beliefs are held about the future. Quite the contrary. Belief in some imminent and radical change to the whole fabric of society may stir people to revolutionary action; belief in some ultimate but distant judgment may serve to reinforce existing rules very effectively. Beliefs in the future, that is to say, may have a powerful social function, which can be either revolutionary or conservative. They may be quite loosely related to a group's other beliefs about the will and nature of God. What I am asserting is that a group's beliefs about the future can be substantially modified without that group's losing its overall sense of continuing identity.

What is interesting about the Pharisees is the constantly changing nature of their hopes. They started out in life as a part of the Hasidaeans, fired by the Danielic hope of the coming of the Kingdom of the saints of the Most High. They joined with the Maccabees in fighting a successful war against the Seleucid dynasty in Syria. They then sought, ultimately unsuccessfully, to implement their vision of society through the Hasmonean court. Under the Romans they began to consolidate their power base in the local communities in Israel, while still contending for power in the Sanhedrin at Jerusalem. At the time of the Jewish War in 66–70 A.D. they fought, admittedly reluctantly, against the Romans, as hopes again rose of a Jewish national state. Thereafter with the loss of position of the priests after the destruction of the Temple, they assumed leadership of the people in the academy that developed at Jamnia under Johanan ben Zakkai. From then onward it is reasonable to assume that their hopes for radical change receded more and more, while their efforts were directed toward laying the foundations of a new form of Judaism based on individual and communal piety.

Thus if we ask what the function of beliefs about the future was within Pharisaism we must expect a complex answer. The fact is that at some periods of their history such beliefs may have stirred them to revolutionary action against occupying forces; at other times they may have served to console them in the face of their dashed hopes for national independence. Certainly the later literature has a somewhat pensive character when it speaks of Jewish hopes. But if we speak of the period after the fall of Jerusalem as wistful in respect to its hopes for some future age of Jewish independence and world rule, we must not lose sight of the fact that this was also a period when the rabbis were actively engaged in developing the new forms of Judaism that were about to take it through the next two thousand years. Wistfulness about past hopes does not necessarily mean present inaction.

The Essenes

The Pharisees, we have just seen, embraced a number of hopes for the future in the course of their long history. Much the same is true of the Essenes.

Like the Pharisees, the Essenes have their origins in a time of high expectation of radical change during the Maccabean revolt (166–159 B.C.). Initially they saw the Maccabean revolt as the prelude to divine salvation. Unlike the Pharisees, however, they broke early with the Maccabees and were thus forced to revise their initial hopes, which they then regarded as mistaken. Under a new leader, the Teacher of Righteousness, they retired to the desert to "prepare the way of the Lord" (Is 40:3 quoted in 1QS 8.14), expecting, that is, some imminent act of divine intervention. When these hopes for an immediate resolution to Israel's oppression were in turn disappointed they were not so much abandoned as rescheduled. The text of Isaiah then referred not so much to the original move to the desert as to each individual member's decision to separate from the rest of Israel and to study the Law according to the teaching of the community.

Much of the subsequent life of the community must have been concerned with developing its own rules and discipline. At the same time it was still occupied with questions of God's Rule over history and never abandoned its hope in some liberation to come. One of the features of the community's own writings was the concern to interpret the "times." Prophetic texts from the Old Testament like Habbakuk were worked over verse by verse and related to the present circumstances of the community (1QpHab). In this way the community was able to plot its position in the overall divine plan.

Another feature of the Essene writings is the development of visions of the future. These again vary in detail and complexity. In the Community Rule a fairly simple account of the final "visitation" is given (1QS 4.6–14): Those who walk in the spirit of truth will receive "healing, great peace in a long life, and fruitfulness, together with every everlasting blessing and eternal joy in life without end, a crown of glory and a garment of majesty in unending light" (6–8). By contrast, the visitation of those who walk in the spirit of darkness shall be "a multitude of plagues by the hand of all the destroying angels, everlasting damnation by the avenging wrath of the fury of God, eternal torment and endless disgrace together with shameful extinction in the fire of the dark regions" (1QS 4.11–13). It is a vision of some final judgment where the wicked will be consigned to the fire and eventually destroyed; the righteous, on the other hand, will enjoy a long period of this-worldly prosperity followed by eternal bliss. In all this the document draws freely on the Old Testament and other writings of the time (1 En.). What is new of course is that in these prophecies the just are identified with the community; those under judgment are identified with all others, Jews and Gentiles. There is, however, no specific reference to the immediate political circumstances of the time; it is more an assertion that God will ultimately vindicate the community and put its enemies to shame.

By contrast, the War Rule, another major text of the community, contains many more specific references to the Roman occupation of Palestine and looks forward to a final battle between the sons of darkness and the sons of light. The sons of darkness are variously identified with the forces of the Kittim (the Romans), the Assyrians, and the sons of Japheth and many others. A detailed campaign is described that will ultimately be resolved by "the mighty hand of God" (1QM 18.1). The work is full of instructions about the ordering and military tactics of the sons of light, which seem to reflect contemporary Roman military practice. Yet it is far from being a simple army manual. It is clearly a visionary work that predicts the ultimate global triumph of the community – a bold vision indeed.

This is not all. There are references elsewhere to messianic figures: a prophet and two messiahs, one priestly and one kingly (1QS 9.11). The reference to the prophet seems to derive from Deuteronomy 18:15, where the rise of a prophet like Moses is predicted. The notion of two messiahs is unusual but has antecedents in the Old Testament: Haggai 2:23; Zechariah 4; 6:9–14. The idea is found also in another Qumran document, a collection of scriptural quotations, 4QTestimonia. The community may have originally expected a priestly messiah, associated with the Teacher of Righteousness who was himself a priest. Subsequently this was perhaps fused with the more traditional belief in a messiah after the manner of King David. Interestingly the priest-messiah is to take precedence in matters of ritual and doctrine. This suggests something at least about the community's views of what the proper relationship between priest and king should be. It reflects, no doubt, the continuing sense of outrage at the usurpation of the high priesthood by the Hasmoneans.

Again, it is difficult to piece all this together. The diversity suggests that at certain times in the Essenes' history their original expectations of some violent and dramatic end to present oppression could flare up within the community. But equally it is likely that such periods of heightened expectation were not sustained indefinitely and that at other times the community's efforts were directed more to enforcing its own discipline, to maintaining its identity as a minority group on the margins of its society. Here, there were two major preoccupations. In the first place, a certain measure of "rescheduling" of the community's hopes was necessary, in order to preserve continuity in the community's teaching. Second, beliefs in some future judgment, "visitation," were reemployed. Their function was no longer principally to prepare people for conflict and violent death, but rather to reinforce the group's own values, as can clearly be seen from the passage in 1QS 4 where the two "visitations" are linked to a portrayal of two "ways," the ways of the spirits of truth and falsehood. But of course such reemployment of apocalyptic hopes does not mean that hopes for the eventual restoration of Israel and the Temple were altogether lost sight of.

It is therefore not surprising that the Essenes fought and were destroyed in the First Jewish War. Their dreams of overcoming the military might of Rome were shown to be just that – dreams. In the end what Qumran represents is the ultimate folly of a minority culture supposing not only that it can assert its own cultural identity in the face of overwhelmingly more powerful cultural forces but that it can actually impose itself on them by force. Such dreams may have the power to arouse a whole people in times of great pressure. They are hardly a recipe for survival, still less for growth and development.

The Zealots

Contemporary accounts of the Zealots' beliefs make it clear how much they longed for freedom from foreign domination.

Judas the Galilean, we are told, "upbraided the Jews for recognising the Romans as masters when they already had God" (*War* ii.433, cf. *Ant.* xviii.23). Equally they saw the road to freedom as being one that it was their duty to set out upon for themselves in obedience to their only king and ruler, God. Freedom would come as the result of the military overthrow of the Romans.

Yet the way to such victory was not thought to be simple. Nor was it. Not only was it fraught with dangers from those who betrayed Israel and made cause with the foreigners, it meant doing battle with a vastly superior power. Thus the Zealots knew that they would have to suffer. They exalted the model of the Maccabean martyrs and steeled themselves for the worst.

How was it all to end? The Zealots certainly believed that victory over the Romans would not come simply by their own efforts. Their task was to cooperate with God; ultimately the victory would be God's. Did they, again, have any very specific ideas of how this might be?

There are at least indications that they looked for some decisive military intervention on God's part. Whether this was to be in the form of the raising up of some powerful military leader (messiah?) or more in the form of some angelic intervention is not clear. Menahem, one of the Jewish leaders during the First Jewish War, certainly wore royal clothes and gave himself messianic colors (*War* ii.443-4). However, the followers of Eleazar felt this to be an intolerable assault on their liberty and overthrew him before continuing the struggle against the Romans. On the other hand they may have looked for some miraculous intervention, more after the manner of Joshua's victory at Jericho or the deliverance of the Israelites at the Red Sea. Thus we hear of one Theudas (Acts 5:36) who led out a large band in the expectation of seeing the waters of the Jordan parted. His group was attacked by Roman cavalry and

Theudas was beheaded (*Ant.* xx.97–9). One way or another, they believed, the time for decisive divine intervention would come. Could they influence its coming?

Again there is little to go on. The main clue seems to be that the Zealots at least believed that God would not intervene *unless* they took up the military struggle. Thus Josephus says the Zealots believed "that heaven would be their zealous helper in furthering their enterprise only if they actively co-operated in the matter, all the more if with high devotion in their hearts they stood firm and did not shrink from the hardship that great aims require" (*Ant.* xviii.5). It is then probable that they also believed that there was a sense in which their efforts would help to "bring in the end," a notion that is found also in the rabbinic tradition (Cant.R. on 2.7) where it is also linked with the idea of overthrowing the Romans. In practice this could only be a relatively imprecise expectation. Its importance would be more that it would strengthen those undergoing particularly severe suffering. The thought would be there that the more they suffered, the nearer they would bring the desired end. Certainly those who fought in the cause of Jewish national freedom in the first century were not short of opportunities for such suffering.

What then ultimately did the Zealots hope for? Here we encounter again that interesting mixture of the concrete and the wholly fantastic that characterizes many such hopes. On the one hand it is clear that they looked for the restoration of Jewish national sovereignty. The accounts of the burning of the money lenders' bonds in A.D. 66 (*War* ii.427) also make it clear that the Zealots wanted to rid the people of its accumulated debts. Like Judas Maccabeus they will have hoped to restore the Temple to its former glory. All this remains firmly within the bounds of the historically possible. But there are other features that suggest that their hopes extended beyond this. The hope for some final intervention on God's part recalls passages like the Sibylline Oracles 3.669–701; 1 Enoch 90.16ff. The readiness to accept martyrdom (*Ant.* xviii.23–4) and to commit suicide (*War* i.313) again suggests that their hopes embraced more than this world. Like the Maccabees they expected the resurrection of their heroes (cf. 2 Mc 6:24–30; 7:7–14). It is almost as if they knew that the final liberation could never be achieved under the present conditions of this world. Some more radical transformation was needed that would make possible lasting freedom and peace.

John the Baptist and the "Prophets"

The groups we have been looking at so far all had their own programs of action and a recognizable history. Around the time of Jesus, however, we find figures who emerge for a short period, gather a crowd of followers, and then disappear more or less from view. Such movements appear to focus on a prophecy of some quite specific act of divine intervention.

John is one such figure. He emerges during the reign of Herod Antipas (4 B.C.–A.D. 39), proclaiming the imminent coming of the "stronger one" who will bring judgment and salvation (Mt 3:1–12). The important thing for people to do is to prepare themselves for this coming crisis. "Repent and be baptized." Certainly once baptized they are to "bear fruits worthy of repentance." But that in a sense is only to show that they have truly repented and so will be baptized with spirit and not with fire. So great is the imminence of the final crisis that all earthly programs are irrelevant. The important thing is to show that one's heart is ready for the coming age that God will bring in.

What did John expect to happen? The mightier one who will come "will baptize you with the Holy Spirit and with fire. His winnowing fork is in his hand, and he will clear his threshing floor and gather his wheat into the granary, but the chaff he will burn with unquenchable fire" (Mt 3:11f.). John's expectations, at least as we know them, are concentrated in two terrifying images: one of the ax resting against the trunk of the tree ready to rise and strike at its base (3:10); the other of the winnower, tossing the grain on his shovel and separating chaff from the grain, ready for burning. The terror of these images lies in the harsh application of agricultural implements to the fate of the souls of men and women. But at least beyond the terror lies the hope of being gathered into the safety of the eternal harvest.

John was not alone in proclaiming a sudden and dramatic end to the present age. Josephus records a number of other prophets who had similarly vivid expectations: a Samaritan, Theudas, and the Egyptian (*Ant.* xviii.85–8; xx.97–8; 169–72; cf. *War* ii.261–3; the latter two figures are also referred to in Acts 5:36 and 21:38). What is characteristic of these figures is that they expected some divine or supernatural act that would usher in the end time. The Samaritan (A.D. 35) expected the discovery of the sacred vessels of the Temple on Mount Gerizim. In the Samaritan's eyes this would have established him as the Messiah. Theudas (between A.D. 44 and 46) persuaded a large crowd to follow him to the Jordan where he would part the waters as Joshua had done before (Jos 3:15ff.). The Egyptian (between A.D. 52 and 60) collected a large band in the wilderness that he intended to lead to the Mount of Olives. There they would witness the fall of the walls of Jerusalem and would enter and possess the city.

Fairly clearly such figures invoked glorious events of deliverance in Israel's past to arouse hopes for present liberation. In the case of the Egyptian these were certainly related to military and nationalistic hopes. As Joshua had taken Jericho, so the Egyptian would take Jerusalem from the Romans. The same is more than likely to have been true of Theudas. Like Joshua he would enter the land miraculously to reclaim it from the occupying powers. That is to say, these are signs that are in part intended to give credence to would-be Jewish liberation leaders, in part seen as inaugurating the process of liberation itself.

There are interesting similarities and dissimilarities between these signs and John's baptism. All mark the beginning of the end. All, that is, are in a sense messianic. But Theudas and the Egyptian are more clearly military figures whose aspirations were political. They sought a restoration of Jewish national sovereignty. While John may have encouraged Roman soldiers to repent, Theudas and the Egyptian were hell-bent on their destruction.

More important, while the Egyptian's and Theudas' hopes were clearly definable in this-worldly terms, John's were not. John's images of the ax and the winnowing shovel, like Death's scythe, speak of some radical end and new beginning. The face of the earth will be changed – or indeed it will pass away and yield to an entirely new world.

Thus Josephus' prophets stirred men to rise up against the Romans and they were met with determined, sometimes heavy-handed, resistance by the Roman governors. John's movement was not political in this way. Nevertheless his visions of the future had a powerful effect on his contemporaries and were regarded with concern by the authorities. Were they wrong to be concerned? Not entirely. Visions like John's impinge on people at different levels. On the one hand like the hangman's noose they "concentrate the mind wonderfully" and cause people to take stock of themselves. In practice they made John's followers resolve to embrace a new life of just and honest deeds and to turn their back on their old ways. But in another way the effect was to break people's loyalties to the old age altogether. This whole age was condemned insofar as it was about to pass away. And that kind of belief, even though it is not tied to any particular revolutionary program, is in a general way subversive. It encourages people to expect the new; it makes them ready to accept change. When such beliefs become popular, they rightly become disturbing to the authorities. They may prepare the ground for more active political subversion.

Jesus' Hope

Where does Jesus fit into this spectrum? Is he to be numbered among the prophets who expect some imminent and dramatic intervention on the part of God? Or is he closer to the Pharisees and the Zealots, who look to some final act of God to vindicate and bring to fulfillment programs of action in which they are already busily engaged?

Jesus' relation to John the Baptist must at least suggest that he is closer to the prophets. Jesus, as is well testified in the Gospels, was baptized by John (Mk 1:9–11 and parallels). The Gospels offer different accounts of his reasons for this. The most likely is that he was in fact a follower of John and that at this stage he accepted the Baptist's belief in the coming "stronger one." When the Baptist was arrested and beheaded his followers, for the most part, disbanded but the expectations did not simply disappear. Some expected John the Baptist to return (Mk 6:14); many continued to nurse hopes for some coming divine intervention. Among this latter group we may number Jesus.

Jesus' own vision of the future may have grown out of his initial disappointment at the arrest of the Baptist. Alternatively, as some of the gospel accounts suggest (though not, importantly, the Fourth Evangelist's, Jn 1:19f.), it may have sprung from his own baptism by John (Mk 1:11). However that may be, it is clear that Jesus emerges as a prophetic figure in his own right *after* the arrest of the Baptist (Mk 1:14, though contrast Jn 3:24). Perhaps less obviously, his vision of the future was now rather different from that of the Baptist.

At this point we would ideally need to engage in much detailed discussion of the New Testament evidence. Here I can only summarize my views. Jesus certainly looked for some imminent act of intervention on God's part. "There are some of you standing here who will not taste death until they see the Kingdom of God come with power" (Mk 9:1). I am doubtful whether he, any more than John the Baptist, spelled that out in very full terms. The Gospels certainly do. There are full accounts of the events that are to come in Mark 13, Matthew 24 and 25, and Luke 21. In this the Evangelists were drawing on that common stock of hopes on which Jews very naturally drew to flesh out their expectations. It is nevertheless likely that Jesus anticipated some coming figure who would judge and save, whom we now know as the Son of man (Mk 8:38 and parallels: 14:62). Whether Jesus used that phrase as a title is hotly debated.

We may learn more about the nature of Jesus' expectations from his actions than from his recorded teaching on the subject. Jesus went about healing and exorcising. He ate with tax collectors and sinners. He called some people to follow him and appointed twelve with particular authority. He went up to Jerusalem and performed a significant act in the Temple.

How does all this compare with the recorded actions of Josephus' prophets? It is not easy to fit it into any neat pattern of Old Testament associations. Healing and calling disciples would fit with Elijah/Elisha. Elijah was indeed one of the figures associated with the end and this might indicate something of Jesus' own self-understanding as a prophet of the end time (Mt 11:14; 17:9–13). The many exorcisms recorded of Jesus may tell us a little more. Belief in demons and evil spirits is to be found at all times and in all places. What is interesting here is the suggestion that the final age will be brought about by the defeat of Satan. The implication seems to be that this age is at present under the sway of Satan – not just under attack from him – and that only when his reign is broken can the

Kingdom of God come in (but cf. Lk 10:17, where Satan's rule is already broken, and Mk 3:23f., where Satan is said to be bound).

Some kind of triumphal entry to Jerusalem associated with the "purification" of the Temple (Mk 11:1–11) might well evoke echoes of Judas Maccabeus' repossession of Jerusalem and the Temple after its desecration by Antiochus Epiphanes (1 Mc 6). The actual nature of the act that Jesus performed in the Temple is more problematic. Some understanding of the geography of the Temple is necessary.

The Temple was divided into various areas, the largest of which was the Court of the Gentiles. From here the way led to the Court of the Women and the Court of the Priests. Within the latter lay the inner sanctum, the Holy of Holies. The Court of the Gentiles was the place where animals for sacrifices were bought. Here money was changed for the Temple currency that was necessary for the purchase of such sacrificial animals. The whole area was overlooked by the Antonia, the fort garrisoned by Roman soldiers. Jesus appears to have entered the Temple and created a disturbance among the traders there. The action hardly seems to have been a determined attempt to seize control of the Temple, something that would have been quickly stamped on by the Roman garrison. It was rather a prophetic "sign," invoking the coming action of God that Jesus expected.

What then did Jesus' action signify? The traditional view is that it showed that God would come and "purify" the Temple of improper practices and restore it to its original place as a house of prayer. This would reflect some of the visions in the later prophets (Mal 3; Zec 14:21) and seems to be – variously – how the Evangelists read it. Others have argued that the overturning of the tables symbolized the *destruction* of the Temple. The Temple would be laid waste and then miraculously restored and rebuilt. Hopes of this kind are to be found in the writings of the time, notably 1 Enoch 90:28f. Both of these views are possible. The nature of the act and the tenuousness of the evidence make a clear decision impossible. The sayings attributed to Jesus about the destruction and rebuilding of the Temple may favor the latter interpretation (Mk 13:1, 2; Mt 23:38).

On either view, though, what is being expressed is a deep sense of alienation from the center of the Jewish religion. It is the act of a Galilean prophet who longs for the renewal of the nation and sees in the leaders of his people and its central institutions the very seat of corruption that paralyzes the nation.

All of this is clearly in line with contemporary expectations. Jesus expected an act of national deliverance, like that achieved by the great figures of the past, but now to be brought about by the direct intervention of God. There is, however, something quite surprising about Jesus' call of the disciples and his appointment of the Twelve to sit on the twelve thrones of Israel. Here there is a remarkably subversive note. Jesus is asserting that the leaders of the restored Israel are not to be the hereditary leaders of the people – they after all have betrayed the people – but Galilean fishermen and artisans. Jesus is laying the ground for the new people of God who will be the true servants of the King and whose leaders will be the Twelve. We should probably read the call to discipleship in the same light. Like the Zealots, who called people to leave all that they had and to follow them in a holy war against God's enemies, Jesus calls people to follow him. It is a call to the true service of God. Those who follow are those who are truly obedient, true subjects of the king, part of the restored Kingdom that will shortly be established with power.

But while this brings Jesus closer to the Zealots, his meals with sinners and tax collectors point to a quite remarkable difference. The Zealots, we have seen, were inspired by the notion of Phinehas' zeal for the purity of the people. All who were alien or who had dealings with those alien to the nation were to be destroyed. It is difficult to imagine a clearer signal of Jesus' opposition to this kind of policy than his meals with tax collectors and sinners. The kingdom that Jesus expected was to be drawn – in part at least – from those who had failed to live up to the standards of the nation. It was even to include those who had collaborated with the foreign powers who dominated the life of the nation. How could there be a place for such disobedient servants within the Reign of God? How could God establish his rule if people like this were to be included in it? What understanding of God's power and kingship is implied by such dramatic representations of the future Kingdom? How could such power ever survive in the conditions of the real world? It is to these enormous and vital questions that we shall turn in the last chapter.

Chapter 6

Jesus and His Kingdom

So far we have been attempting to show something of the variety of ways in which Jews in the first century responded to pressures on their traditional way of life. Faced with economic, social, and political forces that were eroding their communal life and against a background of a common inherited pattern of beliefs and practices, they produced a considerable range of forms of life, of "parties" and groups within Judaism.

Where does Jesus fit into all this? How far can his teaching, like that of his contemporaries, be seen as yet another variation on the theme of basic Jewish beliefs? How far does he develop new insights and beliefs? Does he, too, devise new ways of defining group membership and of maintaining group standards? Above all, in what sense is his teaching a response to contemporary pressures on the Jewish people?

In all probability, Jesus shared many of the basic beliefs of Jews of this time. It seems to me unlikely in the extreme that Jesus could have effectively rejected standard contemporary Jewish practices and beliefs *without signaling this very clearly*. If he had, for example, rejected belief in Israel's gracious election by God, people would simply not have picked this up unless he had said so loud and clear. The same would have been true if he had ceased to believe in God as creator, or as one, or in the Covenant, in the Law as the revelation of God's will and in Jews' duty to perform works of the Law. And nowhere do we have any evidence that Jesus did any such thing. In this sense then we must see Jesus as a devout Jew of his time.

Nevertheless Jesus obviously provoked considerable opposition among Jews. Not that there is anything so surprising about that in principle. Jews were as capable as any other nation of taking different sides on matters of major importance. Certainly there is no mistaking the hostility the community at Qumran felt for – and had itself experienced at the hands of – the official leaders of Judaism in Jerusalem ("the Wicked Priest," the "Spouter of Lies"). Equally Josephus' accounts of the Jewish War portray the very violent antagonisms between various Jewish groups at the time. Not only was there division between those who sided with and those who sided against the Romans; even among the opposition parties there was fierce dissension. Menahem's murder at the outset of the war is an eloquent example of this (*War* ii.441–48). The fiercest debates and struggles are most often between those who agree on fundamentals but disagree about how to interpret or implement them in detail.

In what sense then did Jesus' teaching and ministry represent an important reenactment of those basic Jewish beliefs? And in what sense did it represent a break with central tenets of Jewish faith at the time? Did Jesus, that is to say, draw out the meaning of those basic beliefs in a way that many of his contemporaries would no longer be able to accept? In such a way, that is, that they would say that he had effectively changed their meaning? It is, for example, possible for two people both to affirm that God is one and yet to spell out the meaning of that belief in ways that are mutually incompatible. In a similar way we may ask whether what Jesus said about God's Rule of his world, his Kingdom, would have been acceptable to his contemporaries.

We can of course offer only a brief outline of Jesus' teaching about the Kingdom. It clearly forms a central part of his teaching, just as the notion of God's kingship is widespread in Jewish traditions, both biblical and postbiblical. In one sense or another belief in God's kingship would have been accepted by all

Jews. It was, moreover, a term that could clearly raise Jewish passions and was closely linked to Jewish aspirations for independence. This is particularly clear, for example, in Judas the Galilean's reported insistence on God's sole kingship (*War* ii. 117–19).

What was the Kingdom? In a word it was no more or less than God's ruling of the world. In that sense it was already a present reality that extended back into the history of Israel and the world and would continue to the end of time. God, so Jews believed, was Lord over history and creation. He exercised his rule by controlling the elements and the nations. In particular he had chosen Israel and through Israel would bring his purposes to fulfillment.

But (and this was a concern for many Jews of the time), there were many aspects of experience that suggested that God's Rule was impeded by dark forces that brought disease, suffering, and disruption to peace and justice. One of the clearest expressions of such a view comes in a document from the first century A.D., the Testament (Assumption) of Moses, in which the Kingdom of God is contrasted with the kingdom of Satan and a vivid portrayal of the latter's overthrow is given (Test. Mos. 10.2). Some such view lies behind the understanding of the devil's power in the Temptation stories (Mt 4:8–10). Qumran also contrasted the dominion of Satan with the dominion of the community (1QM 1.14f.; 18.10f.). Jews longed for a time when God's Rule would be fully realized and Israel's sufferings would forever be at an end. In this sense talk of the Kingdom could become a powerful focus for Jewish aspirations for national sovereignty.

Thus when Jesus spoke about the Kingdom of God "coming with power" (Mk 9:1) he undoubtedly touched on a theme that would have raised strong passions and expectations in his hearers. What, precisely – at least precisely as is possible – did he mean by it? How far did this accord with his contemporaries' beliefs and expectations?

We have already noted certain aspects of Jesus' teaching about the future at the end of the preceding chapter. He looked to some imminent event, when God would intervene to establish his Rule, once and for all. His choice of the Twelve and his actions in the Temple seem to suggest that he looked to a radical refounding of Judaism that would effectively dispossess the ruling authorities and replace them with those who had been marginalized by the alliance between the high priests and the Romans.

In this Jesus would clearly not have had the support of all his contemporaries, least of all of the high priestly party. But this does not mean that, in this respect, he was necessarily recasting basic beliefs about the Kingdom. Other groups, notably the Essenes, looked forward to a time when the Temple aristocracy would be replaced. Admittedly, they expected the Temple priests to be replaced with other priests. If Jesus looked forward, let us say, to subordinating the Temple priesthood to the Twelve, then of course that would say something much more fundamental about the nature of God's Rule and the place within it of the Temple cult. But there is no actual indication of anything of the kind. We simply do not know enough about the details of Jesus' future expectations. Indeed even if he in fact entertained such notions that would not in itself constitute a total break with traditional Jewish beliefs and practice.

Nevertheless, such information as we have does allow us to make an important comparison with the other prophetic figures of the time, John the Baptist, Theudas, the Egyptian, and others who looked for an imminent act of divine intervention to resolve Israel's problems. It is characteristic of such figures that they are able to arouse powerful hopes for deliverance in an oppressed and disheartened people. They awake a longing for national renewal and restoration and stir in people an awareness of their own worth and value, encouraging them to break with the old order, which devalues them, and to reach out for the new age, which will bring them release and fulfillment.

Such hopes and expectations of renewal are, obviously, clearly linked to the specific expectation of some dramatic event by which God will usher in the new age. They are *not* tied to a particular program of political action. This is not to say that the prophet's followers may not be required to act – to follow him, to perform certain significant actions; only that such actions will not be played out in the conventional political terms of the day. They are the actions of those who are politically marginalized, cut off from the main arenas of power. Nevertheless, they do powerfully articulate their hopes and aspirations.

Such prophets come and go. The hopes they so quickly arouse may be as easily dampened by the disappointment that follows the nonappearance of the promised event. This does not, however, necessarily mean that they leave nothing of significance behind: Where they may make a contribution of, on occasion at least, world-historical importance, is in the articulation of new values and assumptions about power. For the great prophets are possessed, not simply of some hope for an immediate end to this world but of a vision of the future, of a new world with new values, a new humanity, new possibilities for peace and justice. It is in the articulation of such values that they become, in Shelley's phrase, the "unacknowledged legislators of mankind" and bequeath to their followers a task – of seeking in their ever-changing circumstances to embody those values in new communities and societies.

Where do we find expressions of such values in Jesus' teaching? There is, first, a certain amount to be learned from his explicit teaching on ethical matters. Jesus forbade divorce (Lk 16:18; cf.

Mt 5:32; 19:9), encouraged people to treat each other with respect and dignity (Mt 19:18–19), and, perhaps most remarkably, enjoined them to love their enemies (Mt 5:44). Judaism had a long tradition of emphasizing the importance of love and compassion in the dealings of God with his people and of his people with each other. Jesus specifically quotes Leviticus 19:18 in his summary of the Law at Mark 12:29ff. It is a great mistake, that is, to think of Judaism, even that of the Pharisees, as essentially legalistic. Judaism was concerned with the establishment of a world of peace and justice within which people would be free to worship God and to live in harmony with each other. And in this the Law had an essential role to play.

But this is not to say that there were not tendencies within Judaism that, particularly in times of national stress and crisis, emphasized the importance of maintaining tight boundaries between different types of people within the group and, above all, between the group itself and outsiders. We have seen this in Qumran and to a lesser extent with the Pharisees in their use of purity regulations. Thus in emphasizing the need to love one's neighbor as oneself, not to look down on others and despise them (Lk 18:9–14), in summarizing his teaching about the Law as doing to others what you would wish them to do to you (Mt 7:12), Jesus was using the tradition to counteract more rigid and hierarchical views of society. The laws, one might say, are there to provide a framework within which to live harmoniously together; they are not intended to help one to put distance between oneself and others, so to regulate human intercourse that one stifles all spontaneity and warmth.

Jesus, that is to say, longed for a world in which it would be possible for people to deal openly with one another, respecting each other fully as persons. Even his teaching on marriage and divorce should be seen not as introducing harsh regulations to torment the unfortunate, but as emphasizing the potential of the marriage relationship for allowing people to develop deep trust and mutuality. What he was objecting to was the right of a man to dispose of his wife if she offended him.

The point is worth drawing out a little. The debate between Shammai and Hillel (m.Gitt. 9.10; see also Chapter 4, this volume) was about what constituted permissible grounds for divorce, about what, in male eyes, was properly insupportable. They assumed that there were, or might be, things so offensive that divorce was justified. In the light of such discussion, Jesus' prohibition of divorce may be seen as challenging a man's right to dispose of his wife by denying that there are offenses that are unforgivable. This is consistent with the emphasis on forgiveness in Matthew 18:22. Matthew's exception (Mt 5:32; 19:9) is more likely to have been a later concession to his own Jewish community than Jesus' own watering down of his radical ethic.

In all this Jesus was drawing on values and beliefs widespread in the Jewish tradition. His injunction to love one's enemies, however, stretched his links with that tradition to the breaking point. "Enemies" must refer here not simply to enemies within the fold of Judaism, but more widely to all those outside who, like the Romans, actively imposed their will on the Jews. This certainly represents a major shift in attitudes. True, the Law might be gracious in its attitudes toward strangers (Lv 25:6), and Judaism believed that it had an important role to play in bringing blessing to the Gentiles (Is 60:1–3; Ps. Sol. 17), but the suggestion that one should love one's oppressors, that love for the other should know no bounds of nation and race, was a radicalization of that tradition that must have shocked many of Jesus' fellow Jews.

This needs thinking about. It is not, I think, just that it goes against the grain to love people who are actively working for one's own hurt (though it does). There are deeper theological reasons that can be advanced against Jesus' advocacy of love of enemies. Men and women, so Jews believed, are God's agents in his governing of the world. This can be see most clearly in the role of the Davidic kings. Thus in Psalm 72 the king is God's agent ("Give the King thy justice, O God!") and that means that he will care for the poor and the needy and crush the oppressor, so that peace may abound.

So the Psalmist prays: "May his foes bow down before him, and his enemies lick the dust" (v. 9). Similarly in Psalm 101 the king exults: "Morning by morning I will destroy all the wicked in the land, cutting off all the evil doers from the city of the Lord." This corresponds to a deep strand in Old Testament theology that insisted that Israel had a vital role to play in the setting to right of God's world. But that setting to right involved the active combating of evil and the protection of the weak from the oppressor. In thus countering evil and oppression, people were reflecting and indeed collaborating in God's governance of the world. The issue is raised with all due clarity by a matter that must exercise all Jewish and Christian theology. The terrible afflictions of the Holocaust are not just something that must be borne, but something that requires an active response on the part of men and women. In light of the failures – or the inability – of the Allies during the war to safeguard Jews, this response may be seen foremost in the creation of the state of Israel and the establishment of a safe haven for themselves by Jews.

Thus Jesus' injunction to love one's enemies appears to run counter to God's just rule of the world where the wicked must perish if the poor and the needy are to be properly cared for. How can the coming of the Kingdom with power be linked to the love of enemies?

The same dilemma seems to be posed by Jesus' rejection of the very idea of purity in Mark 7:15. This is a very complicated subject. Purity regulations (i.e., dietary laws, rules about washing and avoiding impure substances and bodily discharges) are designed to reinforce the boundaries of a society. Jews are to distinguish between clean and unclean food in order to remind themselves of the distinction God has made between them and the Gentiles (Lv 20:24f.). To deny the importance of such food laws is to assert that the distinction between Jew and Gentile is not of ultimate significance in the eyes of God. This is certainly what Paul asserted (Gal 3:28); it is quite close too to John the Baptist's saying: "God is able from these stones to raise up children to Abraham" (Mt 3:9). It also accords with Jesus' teaching about love of enemies.

In all this, then, Jesus seems to be saying something not only about the values that will obtain in the Kingdom when it comes with power but about the manner in which the Kingdom is to be achieved. God's Kingdom is not to be established by creating a tightly bounded society as a defense against oppression but by opening oneself up to the other, however threatening, so that God may include even his enemies in his Kingdom. A strange thing to proclaim at a time of national crisis and oppression!

Further insight into the values of the Kingdom is to be had through the parables. Here Jesus' hearers are offered certain powerful metaphors that will help them rethink their basic understanding of how God rules: "The kingdom of God is like . . . ". Thus in the Parable of the Lost Sheep the way God rules his world is compared to a shepherd seeking out the lost and helpless sheep (Lk 15:3–7).

Metaphors, such as those contained in the parables, invite us to bring together two rather different clusters of ideas and to let them modify and illuminate each other. We can say "Man is a wolf" and learn something both about the voraciousness of humanity and the links between animals and humans. In Jesus' parable it is the world of the caring shepherd on the one hand and that of the received ideas of how God rules the world on the other that are juxtaposed. God, says the tradition, rules by protecting the poor and the needy from the wicked and rapacious. Insofar as they threaten the poor, they must be kept at bay and destroyed. If the wicked repent, so at least important strands of the tradition hold (e.g., Ps 107), then God will deliver them out of their distress. The shepherd was often for that very reason taken as a figure of the king, guarding and protecting his people. But here Jesus points to a specific action that reveals a different facet of the shepherd's work: his seeking out the lost or stray sheep. Here the traditional picture of the shepherd guarding his flock from the attacks of wild animals, which fits very closely the Psalmist's understanding of God's kingship, is being subverted by another image: What of the shepherd's care for those outside the fold? Does he not care as much, indeed *even more*, for these? One is therefore invited to rethink the way one looks at those outside the fold. Are they too not every bit as much in need of God's care, indeed of rescue, as the weak and needy within the fold? One is invited to look again at one's conception of how God rules.

Of course such an emphasis on God's care for those outside the group poses problems that are variously reflected in Matthew and Luke's retelling of the story. How often can one go on chasing after the erring members of the church who threaten to damage its unity and faithfulness to the truth? Matthew's concern is definitely with them. But against more prudent policies of expulsion, he insists that it is God's will that none should be lost (Mt 18:14). Luke is clearly worried about the consequences of allowing sinners into the fold before they have truly repented (Lk 15:3–7; cf. the similar way Luke has introduced the notion of repentance into Jesus' call in his modification of Mk 2:17; Lk 5:32). But to all such questions the parable, as it were, keeps on insisting that a God who really cares for his people will keep on caring for them even if they stray or get lost. And the theological implications of such ideas are extensive.

Jesus then is inviting people to make a major shift in the way they think about God and his ways of dealing with the world.

Images of fatherhood or caring are no longer to be read in terms of more primary notions of law and order and the suppression of evildoers. Rather such images are put to work to challenge people to rethink their understanding of how justice is to be secured in the world.

At one point Jesus' challenge to people to rethink their understanding of God's Rule becomes particularly sharp. This is in his linking of the term "Kingdom of God" with the meals with social outcasts. The term had strong links in Jesus' day with other terms denoting the punishment and destruction of God's enemies (cf., e.g., Test. Mos. 10.2), and this was clearly contrary to the sense Jesus wished to give it. If Jesus was to use such a term he would need to signal very clearly the fact that he had substantially reworked it. This he did by announcing the Kingdom at the same time as he "welcomed," and shared meals with, tax collectors and sinners.

Jesus' use of the term Kingdom of God probably has a deliberate anti-Zealot bias. Galilee, as we have seen, had been at the center of the rising after Herod's death led by Judas the Galilean, whom Josephus saw as the chief exponent of Zealot "philosophy." Judas laid particular emphasis on the kingship of God. God alone was king and leader. Jews as his loyal subjects were therefore to acknowledge no other king but God. They should neither pay taxes nor submit to the Roman census. More positively, they were to cooperate with God to overthrowing the Romans and restoring Jewish freedom. That is to say, for the Jews of Jesus' day the term Kingdom of God would have had strong associations with a military struggle against the Romans for Jewish independence. Why and how did Jesus use it when his own teaching of love for one's enemies seems so clearly opposed to the use of coercive force?

Jesus' reasons for using the term were probably quite simple. It was most likely the term that served most effectively to express Jewish hopes and aspirations. It conveyed their longing for a world where they could worship God and lead their lives according to their traditions, without interference from outside powers. And what Jesus had to say addressed itself precisely to such intimations of a new world.

But there was a problem. The commonly accepted meaning of the term, as we have said, linked it to ideas of military struggle and to the destruction of God's – and Israel's – enemies. Anyone who claimed *without qualification* that the Kingdom of God would soon be coming with power would have been taken to mean that the defeat of the Romans was at hand. Jesus had to cut it free from its links to such militaristic ideas and set up new associations that expressed his own understanding of what it would be like for Jewish aspirations to be fulfilled.

We have already looked at aspects of Jesus' teaching that would have helped to bring out the distinctive sense of what he himself meant by the word "Kingdom." But in terms of signaling a sharp difference in use, his meals with tax collectors and sinners must have had a more dramatic effect. Meals were a sign of fellowship, and of pleasure, joy, fulfillment. Moreover, if as a first-century Jew one made some kind of point about meals in the context of proclaiming the Kingdom one might also trigger further associations. Jews expected there to be a great feast when the final age came (1 En. 62.14; 2 Bar. 29.4ff.; 1QSa 2.11f.). For all these reasons Jesus' meals provided clues to the nature of the Kingdom that he expected. What then did it mean for someone announcing the Kingdom to eat with tax collectors and sinners? At the very least it would have suggested that such people were to share in the fulfillment of Jews' hopes.

Who were they? Tax collectors in Galilee, we have said, were agents of the tetrarch Herod Antipas, who was in turn a client ruler of the Romans. Taxes collected went in part to Rome, in part to pay for Antipas' own programs of building (notably Tiberias and the rebuilding of Sepphoris), the maintenance of his court, and his diplomacy. However much or little Galileans knew about the constitutional position of Roman client rulers, it cannot have escaped their attention that their taxes financed the building of Hellenistic cities, one of which was even dedicated to the Roman emperor. Thus tax collectors were clearly identified with the tetrarch's involvement in the Roman world and symbols of Jews' subservience to it.

Sinners by contrast were strictly those who had broken the law. The term clearly had a wide range of application. Some have suggested that it referred to certain occupations, like prostitutes and shepherds (the latter because they were thought to be exposed to great temptation to graze their flocks on others' fields and to understate the increase in their flocks). At all events, it certainly applied to those who were in flagrant breach of the Law. It was also a term closely associated with Gentiles, such that "Gentile sinners" was close to being a tautology.

What kind of a statement was Jesus making by sharing meals with such people in the context of proclaiming the coming of the Kingdom? In the first place, he was countering the popular belief that the coming of the Kingdom would be attended by the judgment *and destruction* of God's enemies. The Kingdom would not be achieved by military action against the Romans; God would not require the destruction of sinners, but would seek them out and welcome them into the Kingdom. Before or after repentance?

This is the crucial question. Jesus' meals clearly raised opposition. It is unlikely that they would have done so had he shared them with repentant sinners. Equally, it is quite improbable that Jesus believed that God's Rule could be fully exercised where his will was flagrantly disobeyed. But Jewish tradition (e.g., Ps 107) sees repentance as resulting from God's punishment of sinners and his mercy as being directed toward those who *then* repent; Jesus' meals with sinners, by contrast, suggest that repentance will be *consequent* upon the sinners' acceptance by God and that it is in this acceptance that God's grace is to be seen.

This teaching has major implications for the understanding of how God saves. It is by welcoming sinners into the circle of his light and grace; and this involves risk and cost. Strange as this is, it is quite consistent with Jesus' command to love one's enemies.

Such radical perceptions of God's ways with the world lie at the heart of Jesus' preaching. What they would mean in practice is not worked out in any detail. The Gospels themselves give evidence of the way in which the early Christians had to struggle with building a community on such radical insights. Often they would be blunted. Is it possible to summarize what they would mean in terms of membership requirement and group rules, as we did for Jesus' other contemporaries?

Only in a very approximate way. This because, as we have suggested, Jesus does not work out a detailed program for modifying and maintaining Judaism as he knew it. He is much more concerned to encourage Jews to look to a future and radical restoration. Nevertheless some attempt can be made to state what the implication of his teaching might be.

Whom did Jesus accept as members of the Kingdom? The Beatitudes, at least in their Lucan form (Lk 6:20–3), suggest that it is the disinherited, the physically poor, who will inherit the Kingdom. I suspect this is closer to Jesus' intention than the Matthean form (Mt 5:1–12), which concentrates more on the spiritual values of the Kingdom itself. The coming of the Kingdom will involve a radical upheaval of the present power structures and the inauguration of a new world that will restore to the mainstream of life those who feel marginalized. But this does not mean that those who are at present in power will automatically be excluded; it will, however, require a deep reorientation on their part and this will not be easy (Mk 10:23ff.).

What does this mean in terms of membership for Israel's enemies and non-Jews in general? This is more difficult. There is little explicit teaching in the Gospels about the future of the Gentiles. One or two stories suggest that Jesus was certainly open to them (Mt 8:5–13; Mk 7:24–30), but it hardly appears to have been a topic to which he gave a great deal of attention. From his welcoming of tax collectors who, if not Gentiles themselves, certainly collaborated with Gentiles, we may say that Jesus was in principle ready to open membership of the group to all who would accept the invitation. But it would be pressing the details of this too far to say that Jesus himself actually advocated that the Gentiles would share in the Kingdom. Certainly passages like Luke 13:29 and Matthew 8:11 do suggest just that, but this may represent the early church's drawing of its own conclusions rather than the explicit teaching of Jesus. Even so, it seems to me to be in line with what Jesus was saying.

The question of what Jesus taught about maintaining group standards is again difficult to answer directly. Scholars have long argued over the question whether Jesus' ethical teaching is specifically intended to relate to the coming Kingdom or simply to the intervening period before its consummation. I suspect that this is a false alternative. In some cases where Jesus was asked to rule on matters of pressing contemporary concern such as divorce or tribute (Mk 10:1–12; 12:13–17), he gave answers in just such terms. On other occasions he spoke more generally, but it is not easy to say how far such statements apply to the present or the future consummation. His command to love one's enemies clearly would be inapplicable in a world where God's Rule was unchallenged and obeyed by all. Yet it is by no means irrelevant to Jesus' coming Kingdom. For the Kingdom will be achieved only through the close encounter with God's enemies.

But it is not only that the command to love one's enemies

relates to the means by which the Kingdom will be achieved. It also expresses something about the central nature of God's Rule, the way he exercises his power. Here Jesus seems to concentrate attention on that essential nature of God's will and to offer a final coda, as it were, to his summary of the Law (Mk 12:28–34). Thus we could say that at a time when Jews were finding it difficult to maintain their traditional mores, Jesus, like John the Baptist and indeed the Zealots, radicalizes the demand. He concentrates the demands of the Law, focusing on that which is above all necessary: love of God, love of neighbor, love of enemy.

If in this sense Jesus meets the pressures on Jewish observance of the Law by concentrating its demands in a quite radical way, to what extent did he devise strategies for its implementation? Here we must say something about Jesus' relation to his followers. In so doing we have to distinguish between those whom he called to follow him and those to whom he preached but who continued to lead their normal lives. In the first place Jesus called disciples to follow him in an itinerant, mendicant way of life, preaching, healing, and exorcising. Such a way of life involved making a clean break with one's existing patterns of life and relationships (Mt 8:18–22). The command to leave the dead to bury their dead, deeply shocking to the ancient world, expresses very dramatically the sense in which Jesus required his close disciples to cut themselves off from the existing order of things. And this is of course a very effective strategy for enlisting people's loyalty. Commitment to one set of values is reinforced by a positive act of renunciation of old ways.

All this interestingly distinguishes Jesus' relationship to his disciples from that of the later rabbis to theirs. Rabbinic disciples were not so much called, they rather sought out the rabbis, and what they sought specifically was to learn more about the values that lay at the heart of their own community. In this sense, while they may have had to leave home to go and live near their teacher, the break with their communities was only temporary.

On the other hand Jesus' call to discipleship does resemble that of the Zealot leaders in two interesting respects. In the first instance both figures like Judas the Galilean and Jesus issued an inspired call to people to "go after them." And that call entailed in both cases making a radical break with existing ties in order to engage in a wandering style of life. There of course the similarities cease. There is a world of difference between the guerrilla life-style of the Zealots and the preaching and healing of Jesus and his disciples.

Perhaps the closest similarity is with John the Baptist. He too appears to have had a close circle of disciples alongside the mass of his followers who were baptized and presumably returned home. Where the strongest contrasts come is again in the life-style. Whereas John's life-style is a strongly ascetic one, expressing an attitude of repentance in the face of the coming of the "stronger one," Jesus' is a joyful one, leading his critics to characterize him as a "glutton and a drunkard" (Mt 11:9). It expresses less repentance in the face of impending judgment, more a rejoicing in the grace of God's Rule, which is already being experienced; and this very exuberance generates a particular form of commitment.

In what sense then was Jesus' teaching a response to the pressures that bore on first-century Judaism? In the simplest terms, it was a prophetic response, the vision of a man standing on the edge of his society and looking beyond to a future world. It was a vision that in one sense was disjointed, composed of images, of a messianic banquet, of the Twelve sitting on twelve thrones, of the Temple destroyed and rebuilt, which are simply juxtaposed without possibly any great overall cohesion. In another sense it was fired by deep theological and moral intuition that remains as a challenge to all who hear it. It speaks of a

God whose power resides not in acts of coercive force but in the readiness to search out and win over those who have strayed from the ways of justice and peace.

As such Jesus' prophetic vision may seem a strange response to the problems of dealing with a powerful colonial force that threatened to undermine the Jews' traditional way of life. It certainly was not a serious *political* response to that threat. Neither Jesus nor his followers had the kind of power required for making such a response. Nor was it, in the long run, to make any serious contribution to the resolution of the problems of Jewish nationalism in Palestine. Jesus himself put too much distance between his "Kingdom" and the aspirations of Jewish nationalists for him to have been able to make a contribution there.

Jesus' teaching, it seems to me, responded to his contemporary situation at two points. First, he clearly gave expression to the longings of his own people for release from their trials. This was part of the reason why people flocked to him, and why some were willing to follow him. And it may well have contributed in the long run to preparing the people for some kind of change, even if of a kind very different from that envisaged by Jesus. In this sense Jesus may well have constituted an, albeit indirect, threat to order. Second, Jesus' teaching also has to be seen as a contribution to the wider search for new cultural and social forms of life that the creation of a united Mediterranean world had inaugurated. His vision of a new world based on the power of love to heal, to restore, and to reconcile would continue to haunt his followers and to press them to create societies that approximate it more and more nearly.

Conclusion

Our task in this volume has been to set Jesus in his contemporary context. I have tried to show the extent to which he was part of a period of Jewish history in which Jews were struggling to find ways of overcoming the complex pressures on their way of life created by Roman rule and the infiltration of Hellenistic culture.

In their various ways the Zealots, Pharisees, Sadducees, and Essenes were all trying to remain true to their traditions at the same time as they were trying to find ways in which they could adjust to the changed circumstances in which they found themselves. This may have meant adopting an aggressive stance and attempting to remove the obstacles to Jewish independence by force; it may have meant gradually changing the seat of the cult from the Temple to the local community; it may have meant accepting a substantial loss of political freedom in order to preserve the integrity of the Temple cult; or it may have meant emigration and physical isolation. In each case the group was in effect giving the tradition a new form and a new direction, remaining within the basic framework of beliefs and practices but living them out in interestingly and sometimes strikingly different ways.

In order to achieve their goals of sustaining their tradition under pressure such groups needed, we have seen, to clarify their understanding of group membership as well as to clarify the rules of the group and their strategies for teaching and enforcing them. Again we have seen the ingenuity that various groups expended on this task. What emerges indeed is a picture of a vigorous community, clearly under pressure, responding with considerable resourcefulness to the threats to its traditions.

Jesus, I have suggested, is to be seen as part of this process, but nevertheless as standing on the edge of it. He belongs more to the group of prophetic figures, John the Baptist, Josephus' prophets, who do not seek strategies for preserving the tradition or removing obstacles to its continuance, but instead look forward to some divine act of intervention that will resolve Israel's problems. Prophets like this performed signs or actions that prepared the people for a divine act and that were in a sense designed to bring it about; often such actions alluded to the great saving acts of the past. What this expressed was the deep longing on the part of their followers for deliverance from their plight, their hopes for a new age where God would again be with them.

Such prophetic figures may play an important part in the development of religious traditions. They are able to speak for the powerless and the dispossessed. They derive their power over people partly from their ability to give expression to a people's sense of exclusion, of marginalization and oppression ("come to me, all who labor and are heavy laden . . . ") and also partly from their ability to fascinate them with a vision of a future world. They loosen a people's ties to the old world by entrancing them with a vision of the new. Sometimes this may be all too tenuous a vision that quickly palls and loses its appeal; at other times it may continue to fascinate and to claim people's allegiance over long periods. Perhaps it is in just such circumstances of marginalization and oppression that figures can emerge with new visions of a just and peaceable society.

Jesus was such a prophetic figure, and moreover he was one whose vision of the future was remarkably rich and attractive. That it should have appealed to his contemporaries is in a sense strange. Certainly his vision of the Kingdom was rich in ethical and religious insight. On any reckoning the teaching contained in the synoptic tradition is some of the most perceptive and many-sided in ancient literature. But on the other hand it called for people to be open to the forces that threatened them, to love their enemies, just at a time when Jews were under severe pressure from external forces and when it would have been natural to erect barriers against such forces – when indeed many groups were advocating just that. Perhaps the attraction of Jesus' vision lies precisely in the fact that it opens up the possibility of a world in which it is not might and coercive force that ultimately hold sway, but rather the greater power of a patient love that is able to bear all things.

To speak about Jesus in this way, to set him firmly into his contemporary world, may be disturbing to some. It is certainly a far cry from traditional interpretations of Jesus that see him as a heavenly figure come down to reveal eternal mysteries and to found a new religion. Here Jesus' teaching is seen as developing out of first-century Jewish religious thought as it reacts to its environment; it is seen as giving expression to the longings and hopes of a particular section of his community. There is something accidental about it; it need not have been thus.

Yet while this is certainly far from a traditional understanding of the sources of Jesus' teaching, it does on the other hand do justice to what it is to be human. Religious figures, however inspired, are still human, are still people of their age who have to communicate to people of a particular time and culture. They inherit the assumptions of their age and speak to the people of their age in terms they can grasp. Their views and their insights are constrained by their position within a particular culture, and whatever insights they have to convey to us come through the cultural forms they were able and obliged to use. What we need to learn is that such cultures do not imprison their bolder sons and daughters. The human spirit is able to reach out beyond its time to perceive and grasp truths that seemingly lie beyond its cultural horizons.

To say this is neither to affirm that we can make all that Jesus said our own, nor to deny that his existence, for all its contingency, has its place within some overall scheme that transcends the individual histories of particular peoples at particular times. Both these claims deserve more elaboration than is possible here. But some brief remarks, nonetheless.

Of course the fact that Jesus was a first-century Jew must set him apart from us and means that in some ways he will always be a stranger to us. Scholars may struggle to learn more and more about the way his message and life related to his age, but a final picture will always elude them, and what they discern is often unfamiliar and alienating. His understanding of the world, of the nature of disease and natural phenomena is not ours. His ignorance of the technology that so much controls our world was, obviously, complete. His hopes for an imminent transformation of the world were not fulfilled and cannot be easily recast for our day. His dreams were the dreams of those who were powerless to influence the course of the world: Those who read this book may well find themselves on the other side of the division between the powerful and the powerless.

And yet perhaps this very strangeness may help us to see what it is that unites us to Jesus, and him to us. In his very limitations, we may discern his humanity, the sense in which "he is one of us." For we too are children of our, albeit very different, age. Limited by our own ignorance of the world, of the future, we are at best seekers after the truth, never wholly its possessors.

But it is not just that we may discern in him someone who, like us, is limited by ignorance, by chance, by the conditions of his age. As a Galilean prophet who died a barbarous death at the hands of an alien power, he also represents all those who suffer, who experience the weight of oppression and powerlessness. And this is particularly significant, if not always remembered, in a figure who has been canonized by many of the most powerful societies in the history of the world. His story, his victimization is, or should be, an encouragement to the powerful not to forget the powerless and the downtrodden, "the weary and the heavy-laden." In this sense he questions all those views of the world that simply deny the reality of such suffering, refusing to attend to it or to answer its demands. In this way he is at one with the history of God's chosen – and suffering – people from the time of their slavery in Egypt, through the persecutions of Nero's Rome or, more recently Treblinka, Auschwitz, Stalin's purges, southern Africa, and all the killing fields of our fearsomely modern world. His memory is a challenge to all those who deny the suffering and the persecuted a share in our common world, our common humanity.

Furthermore, Jesus does not simply remind us of the dark side of our world that the more comfortable and the powerful seek to conceal from themselves: burning books, controlling the media, manipulating statistics. What he says partakes of the particular wisdom of those who know what it is to be the victims of the powerful in this world. Out of that darkness there comes to the powerful a word that challenges their deepest convictions and philosophies, judging and transforming them: Love your enemies. The suffering people of the world bear within themselves the seeds of its redemption. And such seeds, such words, such prophecies come from those who have attended to the plight of the poor. For here the limitations of their own tradition as well as of those that oppress them may be transcended in a vision that depicts and makes possible new worlds of justice and community.

For it is not the case that in the history of the world's changes and chances, there are no gains, no sense in which the human search for truth, for wholeness, for peace, for God is ever rewarded. To say that men and women are always in search of the truth and never its possessors is not to deny any gains at all. But such gains are hardly won; and they need to be rewon, to be embodied anew in the lives and communities of every succeeding generation. And it is the ability of such visions of the truth to transcend the limitations and conditions of their age that commands our attention. As it may, in the end, lead us not only to discern in figures like Jesus something of the nature of our common humanity but also to glimpse in them the moving of the Spirit that transcends and renews our world.

Suggested Reading and Questions for Discussion

In the following notes I suggest some additional reading and questions that might help to promote clarification and discussion of the views I have put forward. More important than any of this, however, would be for readers to obtain the ancient texts that I have cited through the book. These help one to hear other voices contemporary to Jesus discussing these matters and convey something of the "strange familiarity" to us of that culture now two thousand years distant. As a general question it might be worth considering how distant that is felt to be. Goethe wrote, only two hundred years ago:

> Let him who cannot give account
> Of three thousand years,
> Remain in darkness, unlearned,
> And live from day to day.

Chapter 1

An excellent introduction to the social and religious world of first-century Palestine is provided by G. Theissen's *The Shadow of the Galilean* (London, 1987). There is also much to be gleaned from his *The First Followers of Jesus* (London, 1978). On the general history of the period, and for a detailed series of studies of the cities in Palestine, see E. Schürer, *The History of the Jewish People in the Age of Jesus Christ*, rev. ed. G. Vermes, F. Millar, and M. Black (Edinburgh, 1973–).

Questions

1. What analogies might one find in our contemporary world to the political domination of the Jews by foreign powers from the second century B.C. to the first century A.D.?
2. How far did social divisions in the ancient world correspond to those in our present society?
3. Hellenistic culture in the ancient world made a substantial contribution to social communication and to the cohesiveness of that society. Consider the ways in which all great powers dominate, not simply by the deployment of military and economic might, but by the control of culture: of language, education, and ideas.

Chapter 2

There are good introductions to the various Jewish parties of the first century and their earlier history in Schürer, *History of the Jewish People.* I have tried to sketch out these developments a little more fully in my *Jesus and the Transformation of Judaism* (London, 1980), Chapter 4. For an introduction to Jewish writing of the period, see G. W. E. Nickelsburg, *Jewish Literature between the Bible and the Mishnah* (Philadelphia, 1981).

Questions

1. There is nothing particularly strange about a religion taking different forms while maintaining, fairly consistently, certain fundamental beliefs. Consider the range of beliefs in the religious traditions you know best. What causes can you discern for changes in belief?
2. Why should the dominance of alien powers have posed a

challenge to traditional Jewish beliefs in the Covenant and
the Law?
3. How significant a change in Jewish belief do you consider
the development of belief in resurrection to have been?

Chapters 3–5

As the argument here in each chapter raises particular questions of each of the main Jewish groups, it makes sense to give
a combined reading list. On the Pharisees, there is much to be
learned from the voluminous writings of J. Neusner. *From Politics to Piety* (Englewood Cliffs, N.J., 1973) would probably provide as good an introduction as any. J. Bowker's selection of
texts and introduction in *Jesus and the Pharisees* (Cambridge,
1973) gives a good idea of the issues that exercised the Pharisees and their successors. E. P. Sanders' account of the Pharisees' "convenantal nomism" in *Paul and Palestinian Judaism*
(London, 1978) has done much to correct Protestant misunder-
standings of the group, though it remains on a fairly high level
of theological abstraction and does not attempt to give much of
an account of the more detailed Pharisaic and Mishnaic regulations.

On Qumran there is a vast body of literature. There are good
discussions of the sources for our knowledge of Qumran in
Schürer, *The History of the Jewish People,* and a useful introduction to G. Vermes' *The Dead Sea Scrolls in English* (London, 1987); see too his *The Dead Sea Scrolls: Qumran in Per-
spective* (London, 1982). For a very readable account of the
exploration and excavation of Qumran, see J. T. Milik, *Ten
Years of Discovery in the Wilderness of Judaea* (London, 1959).
Michael Knibb's *The Qumran Community* (Cambridge, 1987)
gives a very helpful commentary on key texts from the community's library.

The Sadducees have been as poorly treated by scholars as by

the ancient sources, which tell us little. It is worth consulting the article in the *Encyclopaedia Judaica*.

There is more on the Zealots, but it is rather technical. The most substantial book is M. Hengel's *The Zealots* (Edinburgh, 1988), which shows what can be done by a combination of a very close reading of ancient texts and a massive knowledge of other contemporary literature. It is an attempt to build up a picture of Zealot theology based on Josephus' account of the teaching of Judas the Galilean. It has been strongly criticized for the way in which it suggests that the Zealots were a cohesive sect throughout the first century. For other treatments see S. Freyne, *Galilee from Alexander to Hadrian: A Study of Second Temple Judaism* (Wilmington, Del., 1980), and R. A. Horsley and J. Hanson, *Bandits, Prophets, and Messiahs: Popular Movements at the Time of Jesus* (New York, 1985).

On the less technical level, Theissen's *Shadow of the Galilean*, already mentioned, conveys a great deal about these groups, indicates where to follow up the contemporary sources, and has a real feel for the period.

On the specific question of hopes for the future, C. Rowland, *The Open Heaven* (London, 1982), is a major study of the apocalyptic tradition that focuses on its visionary character. E. P. Sanders, *Jesus and Judaism* (London, 1985), argues that Jesus' actions have their place within a wider Jewish movement of "restoration eschatology."

Questions, Chapter 3

1. To what extent do the various texts referred to in this chapter suggest that Jewish descent was an essential part of what it was to be a Jew?

2. What grounds did the community at Qumran have for excluding all others apart from themselves – including other Jews – from the Covenant?

3. In what sense did Judas' talk of God as "sole ruler" of the Jews represent a radical shift in Jewish theology?

Questions, Chapter 4

1. Jews under pressure, I have suggested, tended to emphasize certain aspects of the Law rather than others. Consider whether similar tendencies can be discerned in contemporary religious groups that you know.
2. Conservatism in religion is often thought of as simply preserving the status quo. Consider to what extent the Sadducees were concerned to preserve the religion of the time entire, to what extent they had to modify it in order to hold on to their position. What does this suggest about conservative forms of religion?
3. Consider the different uses of purity regulations in Qumran and among the Pharisees. What do these differences tell us about the values of the two groups?

Questions, Chapter 5

1. In what ways can religious beliefs in the future serve to motivate people? Consider this with particular reference to John the Baptist and Josephus' prophets.
2. Why did groups like the Pharisees and Qumran embrace belief in resurrection, while the Sadducees did not?
3. Why is it that religious groups can apparently change their beliefs in the future quite radically without abandoning their other beliefs about God?

Chapter 6

There is a good introduction to the scholarly debate about Jesus' use of the term "Kingdom of God" in B. Chilton (ed.),

The Kingdom of God in the Teaching of Jesus (London, 1984). An important early book is C. H. Dodd, *The Parables of the Kingdom* (London, 1935). I have developed the views here more fully in *Jesus and the Transformation of Judaism*. Of the many books to choose from, two stand out at the moment for me: E. P. Sanders' *Jesus and Judaism*, already mentioned, and A. E. Harvey, *Jesus and the Constraints of Judaism* (London, 1982).

Questions

1. "When religion becomes too closely wedded to the existing forms of social and political life, it betrays its function of social criticism; if it divorces itself from all concern with the affairs of this world, it ceases to be of any use." Is this remotely true?
2. How apposite is the comparison between Jesus and the prophets whom Josephus describes?
3. In what sense did Jesus' association with sinners and tax collectors signal a radical reappraisal of existing Jewish norms?

Significant Dates, Events, and Writings

Date	Greco-Roman politics	Jewish politics	Jewish religion and literature (approx. dates)	Extra-Jewish religion and literature (approx. dates)
538 B.C.		Cyrus issues decree for rebuilding of the Temple at Jerusalem		
333	Alexander the Great defeats Darius III of Persia. Period of Hellenistic power and influence begins			
323	Death of Alexander; his generals dispute his empire.			
302	Battle of Ipsus; Babylonia ruled by Seleucids; Egypt by Ptolemies			
c. 300 (–200)		Judea controlled by Ptolemies	Koheleth (Ecclesiastes)	
295	Etruscans subjected to Rome			
280				Library founded in Alexandria (eventually comprised 700,000 volumes)

		Septuagint – the Greek translation of the Hebrew Scriptures
275		
266	Rome extends rule over central and southern Italy	
264–41	1st Punic War: Rome begins to extend its power over western Mediterranean	
241	West Sicily – 1st Roman province	
222	Rome conquers upper Italy	
219–201	2nd Punic War; Hannibal crosses Alps. Scipio finally victorious. Portugal becomes Spanish province	
200–198		Syrian conquest of Judea by Antiochus III. Period of Seleucid domination of Palestine (–140)
190	Antiochus III defeated by Romans; has to	

(continued)

Date	Greco-Roman politics	Jewish politics	Jewish religion and literature (approx. dates)	Extra-Jewish religion and literature (approx. dates)
	withdraw from western Asia Minor and pay tribute to Rome			
187–175				
175(–163)	Antiochus IV, Epiphanes	Seleucus III institutes policies of greater Hellenization. Strict enforcement of Hellenization.	Sirach (Ecclesiasticus)	
169		Desecration of the Temple by Antiochus	Rise of the Hasidaeans, the Jewish renewal party. Origins of Pharisees and Essenes	
168	Antiochus turned back by Romans in Egypt during his campaign against Ptolemies. Rome defeats Perseus, king of Macedonia at Pydna. Turning point in Rome's struggle for control of East			
167		Banning of Jewish re-	Jubilees; Testament of	

			the Twelve Patriarchs; earliest sections of ? 1 Enoch
166–159		ligion by Antiochus Epiphanes. Temple transformed into sanctuary of Olympian Zeus. Maccabean revolt led by Judas (d. 160) and Jonathan (d. 142)	Foundation of the community at Qumran
146	Destruction of Carthage and Corinth by Rome. Macedonia a Roman province.		
140		Foundation of Hasmonean dynasty under Simon, Jonathan's brother.	
134–104		John Hyrcanus high priest and ethnarch	Disputes between John and the Pharisees; destruction of Samaritan temple on Mt. Gerizim by John Hyrcanus 1 and 2 Maccabees
104		Aristobulus I high priest and ethnarch;	
103–76	Rome suffers heavy defeats in Asia Minor in war against Mithridates, king of	Alexander Jannaeus high priest and king; conquers Galilee	Dispute with Pharisees continues.

(continued)

Date	Greco-Roman politics	Jewish politics	Jewish religion and literature (approx. dates)	Extra-Jewish religion and literature (approx. dates)
	Pontus (88). Sulla eventually regains all that was lost (84)			
76–67	Pompey puts down slave revolt under Spartacus (73–71); 6,000 slaves crucified	Alexandra queen; Hyrcanus II high priest	Pharisees restored to favor at court	Virgil, Roman poet, b. 70 (–19)
67	Pompey clears Mediterranean of pirates	Hyrcanus II king and high priest, deposed by his brother, Aristobulus.		
67–63	Pompey defeats Mithridates (64); invades and occupies Syria (64–3); deposes Antiochus XIII of Syria (64). Syria a Roman province, along with Bithynia-Pontus and Cilicia	Aristobulus II high priest and king; fall of Jerusalem (63); Aristobulus captured	Pompey enters Holy of Holies Psalms of Solomon 3 & 4 Maccabees	Horace, Roman poet, b. 65 (–8)
63–40	Rise to power of Julius Caesar; Conquers Gaul (51); crosses Rubicon (49); defeats	Hyrcanus II reinstated as high priest under Roman governor of Syria		

	Pompey at Pharsalus (48); installs Cleopatra and her brother Ptolemy XIII on Egyptian throne. Caesar sole ruler (45); murdered (44). Octavian and Mark Anthony defeat conspirators at Philippi (42). Mark Anthony joins Cleopatra in Alexandria	Herod declared king of Judaea in Rome (40) Antigonus high priest and king, after seizing power with Parthian support: last of the Hasmoneans (executed 30)	Virgil's *Bucolics* (40). *Georgics* (37)
40–37	Mark Anthony controls East, Octavian the West	Herod the Great rules with Roman support, instituted by Sossius after nomination by M. Anthony. Supports M. Anthony in civil	
37 (–4)	Civil war between Octavian and Mark Anthony; Anthony defeated at Actium (31). Egypt a Roman province (30). Octavian honored with	Philo of Alexandria, B.C. 25 (–A.D. 50), Jewish writer of Greek works of philosophy and theology	Spread of Mithraism, a Persian religion popular in the Roman armies

(continued)

Date	Greco-Roman politics	Jewish politics	Jewish religion and literature (approx. dates)	Extra-Jewish religion and literature (approx. dates)
	the name, Augustus (27)	war. Successfully pleads his case with Octavian (Rhodes, 30 B.C.)		
4 B.C.		Disturbances on Herod's death. Revolt in Galilee; destruction of Sepphoris by Varus. Archelaus appointed ethnarch of Judea, Idumaea, and Samaria; Herod Antipas, tetrarch of Galilee and Peraea; Herod Philip, tetrarch of Batanaea, Trachonitis, and Auranitis.		
A.D. 6		Archelaus deposed and banished to Gaul. Judea, Idumaea, and Samaria under direct Roman rule	Census provokes opposition led by Judas the Galilean and Saddok	
14–37	Tiberius emperor;			
26–36	Pontius Pilate procurator of Judaea	Death of Philip (33); his territory added	Beheading of John the Baptist. Crucifixion	

		to the province of Syria	of Jesus. Massacre of Samaritans by Pilate – leads to his deposition
37–41	Caligula emperor	Agrippa I king over Batanaea, Trachonitis, and Auranitis (37); Herod Antipas deposed by Caligula after his request to be made king; his territory given to Agrippa I [39]	Flavius Josephus b. 37 (–97). Disturbances in Judea and Galilee over Caligula's plans to set up statue in the Temple. Anti-Jewish riots in Alexandria
41 (–54)	Claudius emperor		
44		All territory in Palestine under direct Roman rule	
54 (–68)	Nero emperor		
66–70		First Jewish War; destruction of Jerusalem under Titus, Vespasian's son and future emperor	Josephus captured, moves to Rome where he writes *Jewish War* and *Antiquities of the Jews*; destruction of Qumran (68)
69	Year of the four emperors. Vespasian emperor (–79)		

Deuterocanonical and Nonbiblical Works Cited

Jewish intertestamental writings:

In the Apocrypha:

1 and 2 Maccabees	1 & 2 Mc
Sirach	Sir.
Tobit	Tob.

In J. H. Charlesworth (ed.), *The Old Testament Pseudeipgrapha*, 2 vols. (London, 1983):

1 Enoch	1 En.
2 Baruch	2 Bar.
Jubilees	Jub.
Psalms of Solomon	Ps. Sol.
Sibylline Oracles	Sibyll.
Testament of Benjamin	Test. Benj.
Testament of Moses	Test. Mos.

Tractates from the Mishnah. In H. Danby, *The Mishnah* (Oxford, 1933):

Aboth	m.Aboth
Demai	m.Dem.
Eduyoth	m.Eduy.
Gittin	m.Gitt.
Hagiga	m.Hag.

Jewish prayers: in E. Schürer, rev. G. Vermes, F. Millar, M. Black, *The History of the Jewish People in the Age of Jesus Christ (175 B.C.–A.D. 135)*, vol. 2 (Edinburgh, 1979), pp. 455–63:

Shemoneh 'Esreh.

Rabinic writings: in J. Bowker, *Jesus and the Pharisees* (Cambridge, 1973):

From the Babylonian Talmud:

Berakoth	b.Ber.
Shabbath	b.Shab.
Yoma	b.Yom.

Other rabbinic writings:

Midrash Rabbah: The Song of Songs	Cant. R.
Sifre on Numbers	Sifre on Num.
Tosefta Yoma	T. Yom.

Greek and Latin authors. There are convenient bilingual editions of these in the Loeb Classical Library (London and Cambridge, Mass.):

Josephus, *Jewish Antiquities*	*Ant.*
The Jewish War	*War*
The Life	*Life*
Philo, *On the Embassy to Gaius*	*Embassy*
Pliny, *Natural History*	*Nat. Hist.*

Writings from Qumran. In G. Vermes, *The Dead Sea Scrolls in English*, 3rd rev. ed. (London, 1987):

Commentary on Habukkuk	1QpHab
The Community Rule	1QS

The Damascus Rule	CD
Messianic Testimonia	4QTestimonia
The Thanksgiving Hymns	1QH
The War Rule	1QM

Index